AF479173

Public Notice 3

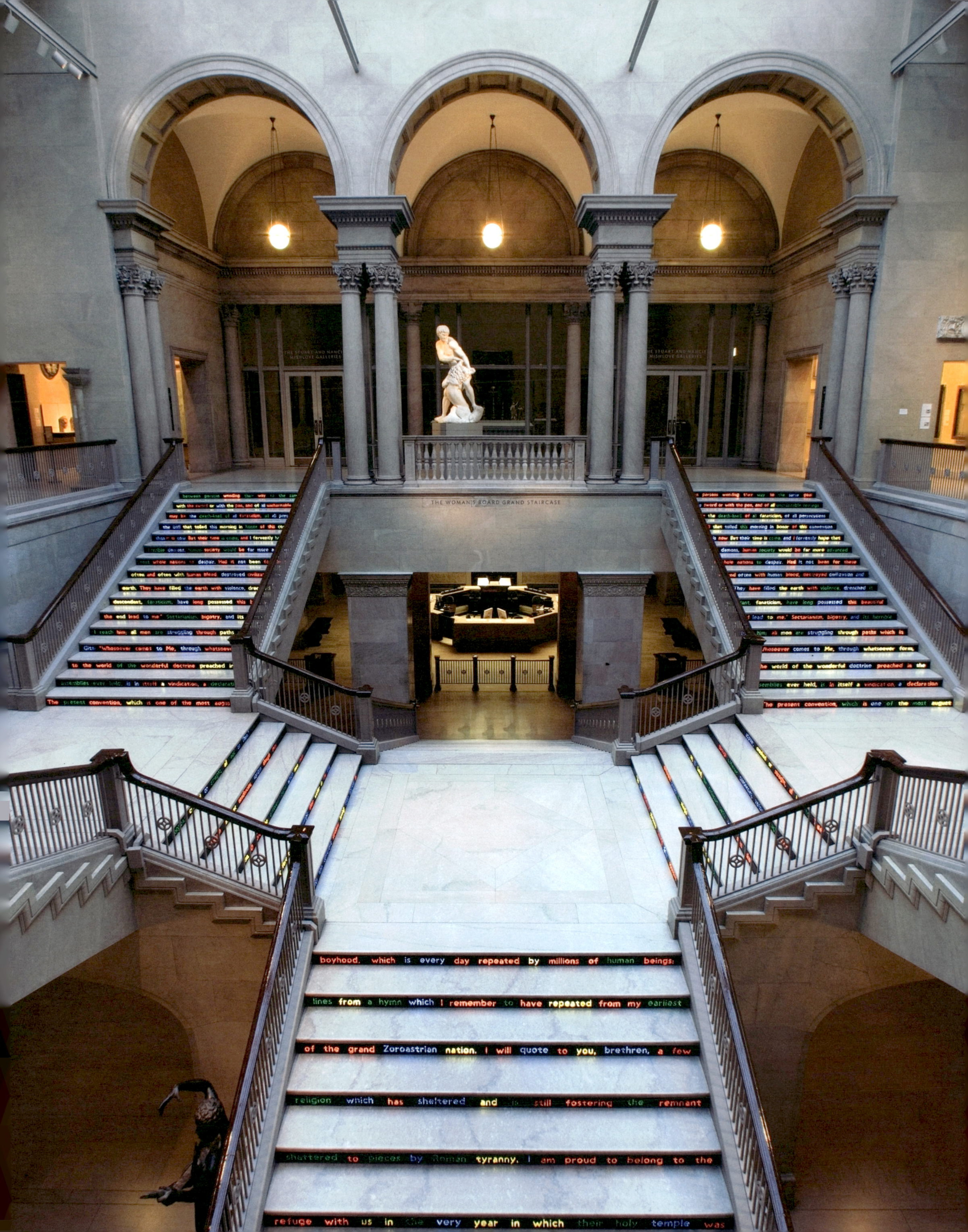

THE WOMAN'S BOARD GRAND STAIRCASE
boyhood, which is every day repeated by millions of human beings;
lines from a hymn which I remember to have repeated from my earliest
of the grand Zoroastrian nation. I will quote to you, brethren, a few
religion which has sheltered and is still fostering the remnant
shattered to pieces by Roman tyranny. I am proud to belong to the
refuge with us in the very year in which their holy temple was

Public Notice 3

Edited by Madhuvanti Ghose

With essays by Madhuvanti Ghose and Shaheen Merali
and contributions by Homi K. Bhabha, James Cuno, Jitish Kallat,
Geeta Kapur, James Rondeau, and Jeremy Strick

THE ART INSTITUTE OF CHICAGO

YALE UNIVERSITY PRESS, NEW HAVEN AND LONDON

Jitish Kallat: Public Notice 3 has been published in conjunction with an installation of *Public Notice 3* on the Woman's Board Grand Staircase of the Art Institute from September 11, 2010, through September 11, 2011.

Lead individual sponsorship is generously provided by Anita and Prabhakant Sinha and the Burger Collection, Hong Kong.

Lead foundation sponsorship is generously provided by an anonymous fund at the Boston Foundation and the Efroymson Family Fund, a CICF Fund.

Individual cosponsorship is provided by Charles and Kathleen Harper.

Additional support is provided by Abby O'Neil and Carroll Joynes, Penelope R. Steiner, Diane and Richard Weinberg, an anonymous donor, Erika E. Erich, Nancy K. and Stuart J. Murphy, and Betty and Richard Seid.

First edition
Printed in the United States of America
Library of Congress Control Number: 2011904325
ISBN: 978-0-300-17158-7 (cloth)

Published by
The Art Institute of Chicago
111 South Michigan Avenue
Chicago, Illinois 60603-6404
www.artic.edu

Distributed by
Yale University Press
302 Temple Street
P.O. Box 209040
New Haven, Connecticut 06520-9040
www.yalebooks.com/art

Produced by the Publications Department of the Art Institute of Chicago, Robert V. Sharp, Executive Director

Edited by Robert V. Sharp
Production by Sarah E. Guernsey and Clo Pazera
Photography research by Joseph Mohan
Subscription and circulation management by Bryan D. Miller and Molly Heyen
Designed and typeset in Trade Gothic by Candice Wong,
Department of Graphic Design
Separations by Professional Graphics, Inc., Rockford, Illinois
Printed and bound by Classic Color, Inc., Broadview, Illinois

This book was produced using paper certified by the Forest Stewardship Council.

This publication also serves as volume 36, number 2 of *The Art Institute of Chicago Museum Studies*.

ISSN: 0069-3235
ISBN: 978-0-86559-245-2 (paper)

For information on back issues, consult www.artic.edu/aic/books/msbooks or contact 312-443-3786 or pubsmus@artic.edu.

Ongoing support for *Museum Studies* has been provided by a grant for scholarly catalogues and publications from the Andrew W. Mellon Foundation.

Photography Credits

Cover, jacket, frontispiece, and throughout: Jitish Kallat (Indian, born 1974, Mumbai), *Public Notice 3*, 2010. Site-specific, text-based light installation on the Woman's Board Grand Staircase of the Art Institute of Chicago; LED bulbs, wires, and rubber; installation dimensions variable. The Art Institute of Chicago, gift of the artist (2010.418).

All works in this publication by Jitish Kallat are © Jitish Kallat. Unless otherwise noted, all works appear courtesy of the artist.

All photographs of *Public Notice 3* were produced by Clare Britt, Department of Imaging, the Art Institute of Chicago.

Photograph on p. 20, fig. 12, © Rusty Culp, Chicago.

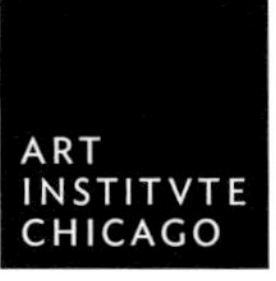
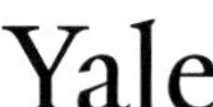

Contents

Public Notice 3 is the first showing of the work of a major contemporary Indian artist, Jitish Kallat, at the Art Institute of Chicago. Jitish's site-specific light installation on the Woman's Board Grand Staircase binds the work into the history of the Art Institute and recalls the visit to this site of the Indian saint Swami Vivekananda in 1893 for the World's Parliament of Religions—a visit that is commemorated nearly every day by Indian "pilgrims" who wish to do *darshan* ("to see" or "behold") on the site of the immortal speech here in this museum—but it also ties it to a subject that is both poignant and relevant to American society as we approach the tenth anniversary of 9/11. It is indeed grimly ironic that the day when Vivekananda presented his "Sisters and Brothers of America" speech full of hope and universal toleration was also September 11, a date now remembered for the horrors of the attack on the Pentagon and the destruction of the World Trade Center towers. *Public Notice 3* opened at the Art Institute on September 11, 2010.

The popularity of the installation has been interesting to watch as we see museum-goers moved by the words of Swami Vivekananda as they walk up and down the stairs; many times we have heard them say that it feels as though the words of Vivekananda were just spoken yesterday—they are still so pertinent and relevant. We thank Jitish Kallat for bringing this important work to us and for gifting it to the museum's permanent collection. I would also like to thank the donors without whom this project could not have been realized: Anita and Prabhakant Sinha, and Max and Monique Burger of the Burger Collection, Hong Kong, for their leadership and support; the Boston Foundation, and Elissa Efroymson and Adnaan Hamid and the Efroymson Family Fund; Charles and Kathy Harper; and Abby O'Neil and Carroll Joynes, Penelope R. Steiner, Diane and Richard Weinberg, an anonymous donor, Erika E. Erich, Nancy K. and Stuart J. Murphy, and Betty and Richard Seid, who all supported the realization of this work at the Art Institute.

I also want to thank those who participated in the global e-conversation over many time zones in the late summer, Homi K. Bhabha, Geeta Kapur, James Rondeau, Jeremy Strick, and Jitish Kallat, for giving up some of their vacation time to make this dialogue possible and meaningful. I also want to acknowledge Shaheen Merali for his stimulating review of Jitish's work.

Internally, I would like to thank Dorothy Schroeder and Karen Manchester for so ably shepherding the project and Maria Simon and the legal department for handling countless details. I am grateful to the Protection Services and Development departments for all that they have done, and am especially appreciative of the efforts of Bernice Chu, Bill Caddick, and their respective departments—Design and Construction and Physical Plant—for enabling us to realize the installation. Robert Sharp and his team in Publications deserve recognition for this splendid catalogue. Finally, I extend sincere thanks to our Alsdorf Associate Curator of Indian, Southeast Asian, Himalayan, and Islamic Art, Madhuvanti Ghose, without whom this project could not have been realized.

JAMES CUNO
President and Eloise W. Martin Director
The Art Institute of Chicago

In the spring of 2009, I met Jitish Kallat at his home in Mumbai and heard from him about his work *Detergent*, which he had recently installed on a staircase in the Guangdong Museum of Art, China, and an odyssey began to try to realize the work at the Art Institute of Chicago. Throughout this effort, our biggest champion remained Julie Walsh, who was present at that initial meeting and who bolstered our spirits with her unending optimism every time our spirits flagged. I must also acknowledge the support we received from Abby O'Neil and Elissa Efroymson in those early days when it all seemed so impossible to achieve. In addition to Julie Walsh, many well wishers helped us in innumerable ways, including Matthias Arndt and Shireen Gandhy, as well as Nina Miall, and I would also like to acknowledge here the immense efforts of Aparajita Jain and her colleagues at Cultivate on our behalf.

I would also like to thank Homi K. Bhabha, Geeta Kapur, Jeremy Strick, James Rondeau, and Jim Cuno for their participation in the e-conversation, which is presented in this volume, as well as Shaheen Merali for his contribution to this book. Homi, Geeta, and Jitish again joined Jim at the India Art Summit in New Delhi on January 21, 2011, on a panel entitled "Forms of Public Address in Contemporary Art," which generated an engaging discussion. We are immensely grateful to them.

Without Larry Smallwood the concept for *Public Notice 3* would never have taken actual shape, and we owe him and the team he brought in from Production Plus in Burr Ridge, Illinois—most particularly Doug Thompson, Frank Weber, and Rick Cruz—a huge debt of gratitude.

At the Art Institute, in addition to Jim Cuno, who believed in this project from its inception, I would particularly like to thank David Thurm and Dorothy Schroeder for their guidance at every stage; Karen Manchester for shepherding the project through; Mary Jane Drews, Lawrence DelPilar, George Martin, Kevin Beck, and Kim Masius in Development; Bernice Chu and Markus Dohner in Design and Construction; Maria Simon in the General Counsel's office; Sally Ann Felgenhauer in Museum Registration; Michelle Lehrman Jenness and the staff in Protection Services; Bill Caddick and his team in the Physical Plant; Clare Britt in Imaging for her photography of *Public Notice 3*; Candice Wong and Jeff Wonderland in Graphic Design; and the wonderful team led by Robert Sharp in Publications. Lisa Dorin provided immense emotional support throughout, and the staff in the Asian Art department—particularly Mary Albert, Craig McBride and Chi Nguyen—helped in countless ways. I would also like to thank my summer intern Nandini Ramakrishnan for her help at a crucial stage, while Abhinit Khanna and Grace Murray provided Jitish and me with immense research support. Reena Saini Kallat has been an incredible supporter from the sidelines from the very beginning. Finally, I would like to acknowledge my immense gratitude and thanks to Jitish for seeing this project through patiently, through all its many ups and downs. What an incredible journey it has been!

MADHUVANTI GHOSE
Alsdorf Associate Curator of Indian, Southeast Asian, Himalayan, and Islamic Art
Department of Asian Art

Acknowledgments

INTRODUCTION

The 1990s were a tumultuous decade in India. Today, after the recent economic meltdown in the West, when everyone is discussing the rise of China and India as economic engines on the world market, it is hard to remember that the Indian state had virtually bankrupted itself by 1991, when under pressure from the World Bank, Finance Minister Manmohan Singh, today the prime minister of India, started a process of liberalization that has opened up the Indian economy and led to an expansion of the middle classes. Singh's measures brought about greater employment opportunities for millions of Indians who could participate in a new way in international markets and take advantage of foreign investments in their native country. This economic renaissance, however, coincided with two major events: the first was the deliberate destruction on December 6, 1992, of the sixteenth-century Babri Mosque at Ayodhya, by a group of right-wing Hindu fundamentalists;[1] the second was the Mumbai bomb blasts of 1993, when a series of bombs exploded within a short period of time on March 12, masterminded by an underworld don, and the resultant sectarian riots in the commercial capital of Mumbai, which led to a kind of awakening from innocence for the Indian middle classes. This convergence of economic upheavals and sectarian conflicts has led to a soul searching within the arts that had never been seen in the post-independence era.[2] In addition, another important anniversary, the 1997 golden jubilee of Indian independence— together with the rise of a certain nationalistic chauvinism and pride—generated a serious questioning of both the horrors that gripped the Indian subcontinent as a result of the 1947 partitioning of India and Pakistan and the enormous migration of peoples that followed that division,[3] and of the present difficulties the country faces, torn once again with sectarian violence.[4]

Against this backdrop a new group of artists emerged in India, commenting on society with a contemporary global voice. Now there was a kind of freedom that artists and writers and filmmakers had perhaps never experienced in the 1940s and 1950s, when the need to resettle in new cities and build life from scratch led to very little commentary and a kind of voluntary national amnesia in the arts about partition. Instead, in the 1990s, in the era of twenty-four-hour news channels, wars and riots were being beamed instantaneously into living rooms and affecting people's consciousness. And Indian art opened up to a field of unlimited possibilities.

JITISH KALLAT AND *PUBLIC NOTICE 3*

One of the artists who emerged out of this milieu in the 1990s is Jitish Kallat, who started exhibiting soon after graduating from the Sir Jamsetjee Jeejeebhoy School of Art in Mumbai in 1996 at the age of twenty-two. In the midst of a vast variety of work from paintings and sculptures to mixed-media installations in his relatively short career (see the following essay by Shaheen Merali), Kallat has also created a series in which he has used historically significant speeches as a commentary on India and the world.

In the first of these works, which he entitled *Public Notice* (2003), Kallat took as his subject the speech that India's first prime minister, Jawaharlal Nehru, delivered shortly before the stroke of midnight on August 14, 1947. Nehru's address, commonly referred to today as his "Tryst with Destiny" speech, was given on the eve

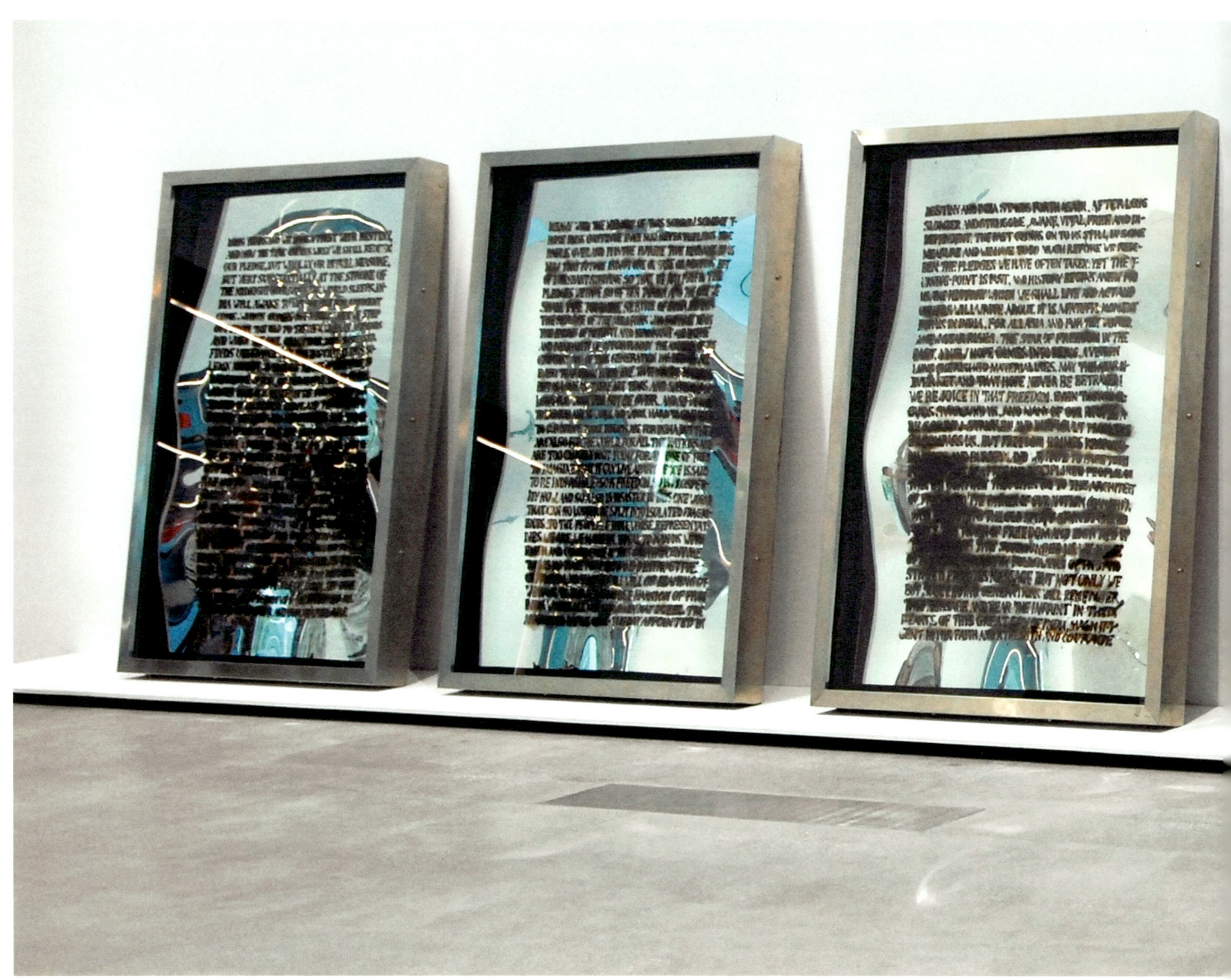

of India's independence, acknowledging that the country would awake to freedom after centuries of colonialism and a long struggle for self-rule.[5] It was a speech filled with optimism and hope for the new dawn of Indian independence, against the backdrop of terrible sectarian violence that surrounded the partitioning of the subcontinent into India, West Pakistan, and East Pakistan (today Bangladesh), with reports of trains full of dead leading to further massacres, and with the concomitant displacement of millions of people. Created in reaction to the horrors of the Godhra riots in Gujarat in February 2002—when train compartments carrying pilgrims were set on fire in Godhra, resulting in riots across the state of Gujarat—*Public Notice* presents the hopeful and inspirational words of Nehru, which were first hand-rendered using rubber adhesive on five acrylic mirrors, before being set aflame, thus incinerating the words and warping the mirrors and their reflected images (see figs. 1–2).[6] According to Kallat, "the words are cremated . . . much as the content of the speech itself was distorted by the way the nation has conducted itself in the last six decades."[7]

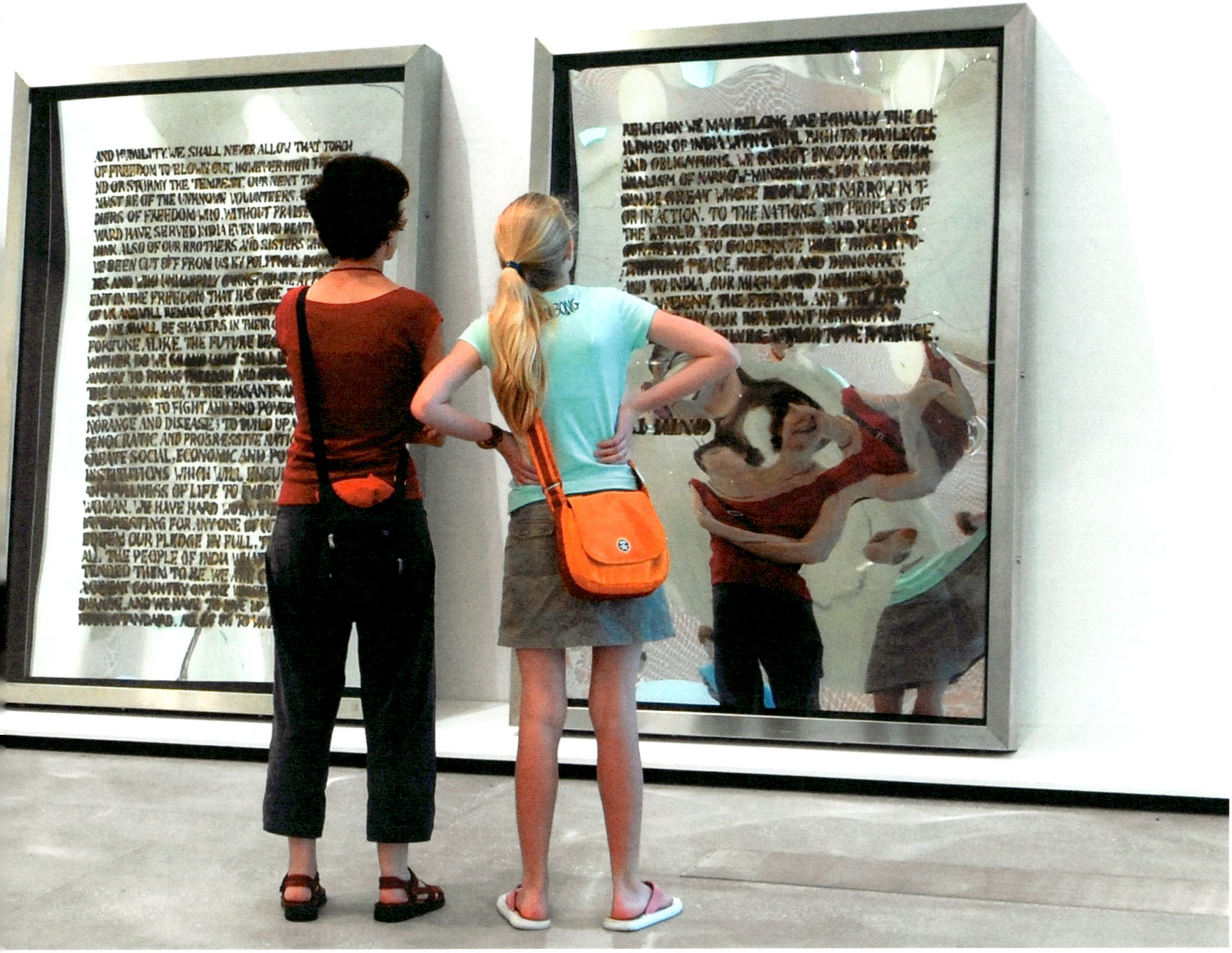

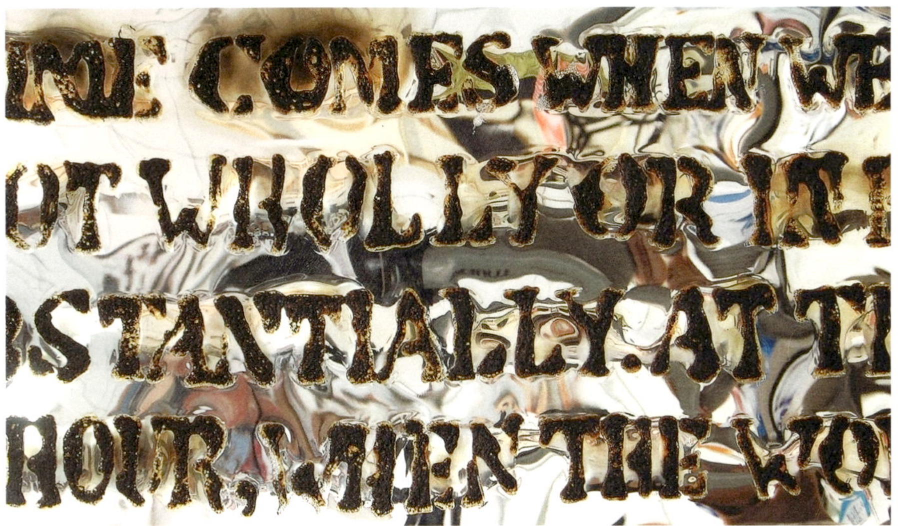

Figure 1
Jitish Kallat, *Public Notice*, 2003. Burned adhesive on acrylic mirror, wood, stainless steel; five panels, each 198.1 x 137.2 x 15.2 cm (78 x 54 x 6 in.). Shumita and Arani Bose Collection, New York.

Figure 2
Public Notice (detail), 2003.

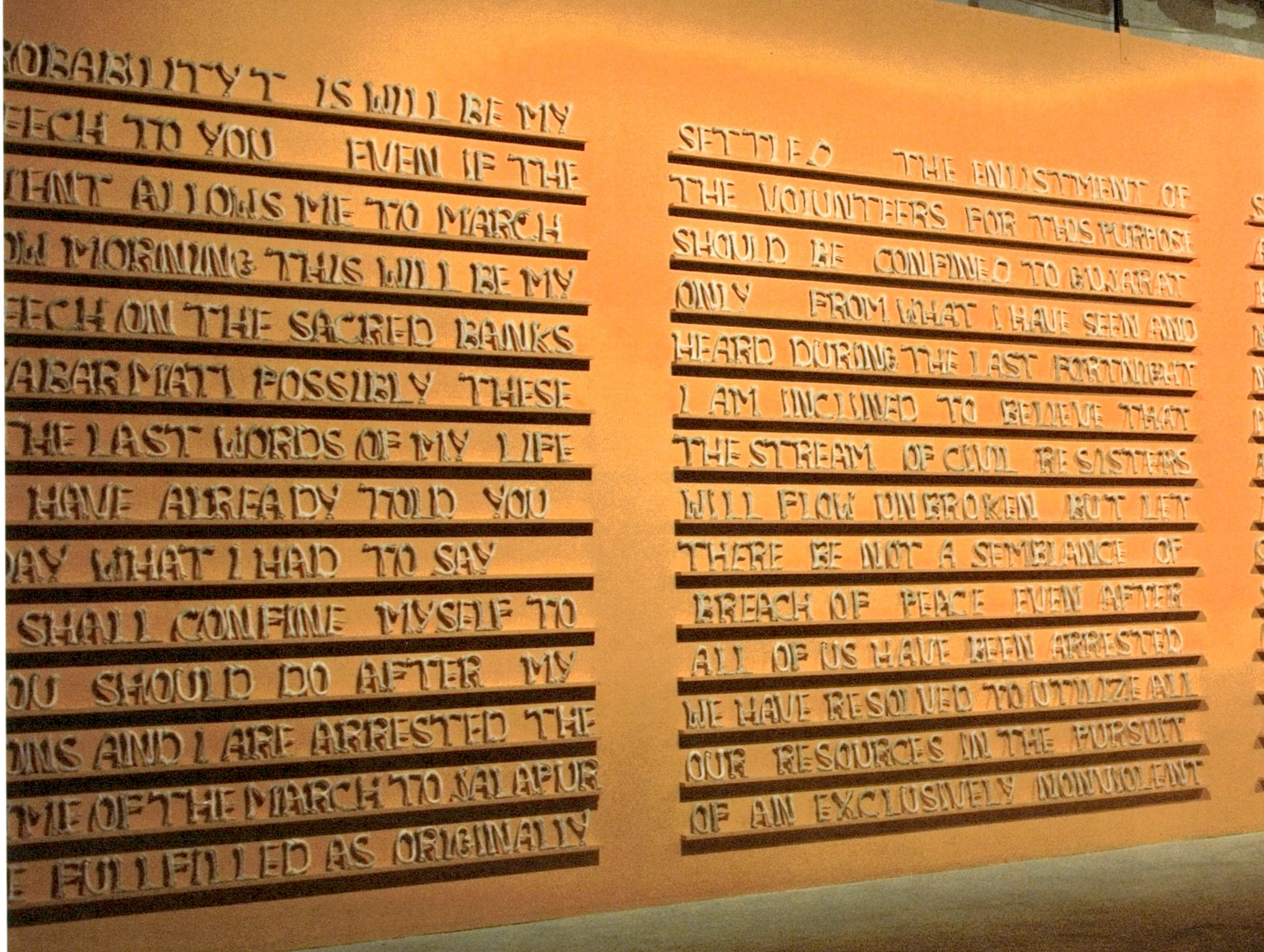

In *Public Notice 2* (2007), first shown at the Hangar Bicocca, Milan, Kallat recreated the entire text of the speech that Mahatma Gandhi gave on March 11, 1930, on the eve of his epic march of approximately 240 miles to the small town of Dandi on the coast of the Arabian Sea—a demonstration of civil disobedience and nonviolent protest that Gandhi would lead to oppose the unfair Salt Tax that the British had imposed on the citizens of India. Kallat wished to remind people of the spirit of nonviolence in a world that was being torn again by sectarian violence, as witnessed in the worst communal riots since partition in the 2002 Godhra riots in Gujarat. In a chilling commentary, Kallat used resin to fashion approximately four thousand five hundred bone-shaped letters of the alphabet to describe what he called, in his own words, the "discarded relics" of the Gandhian spirit of non-violence in today's Gujarat, Mahatma Gandhi's birthplace (see figs. 3–4).[8]

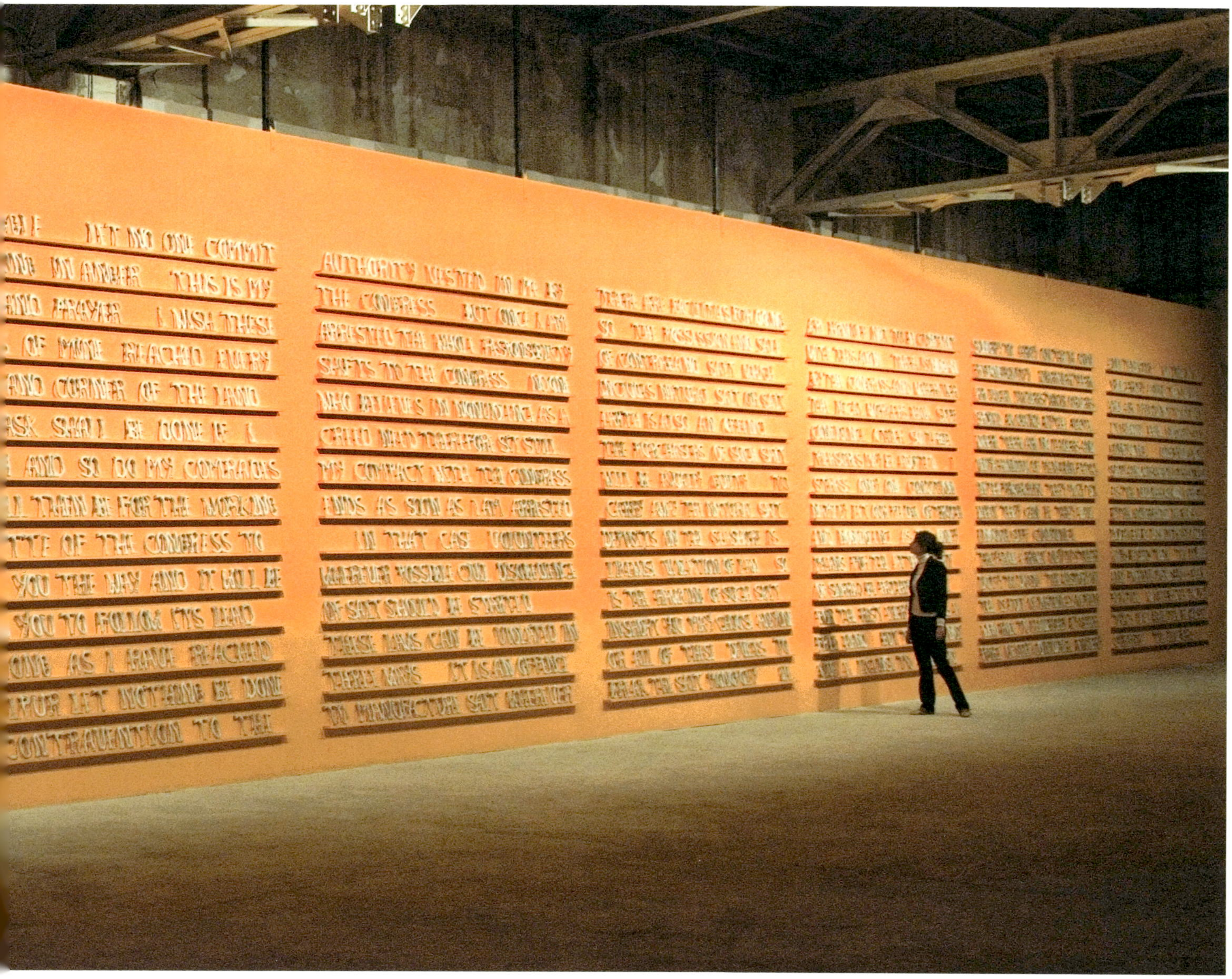

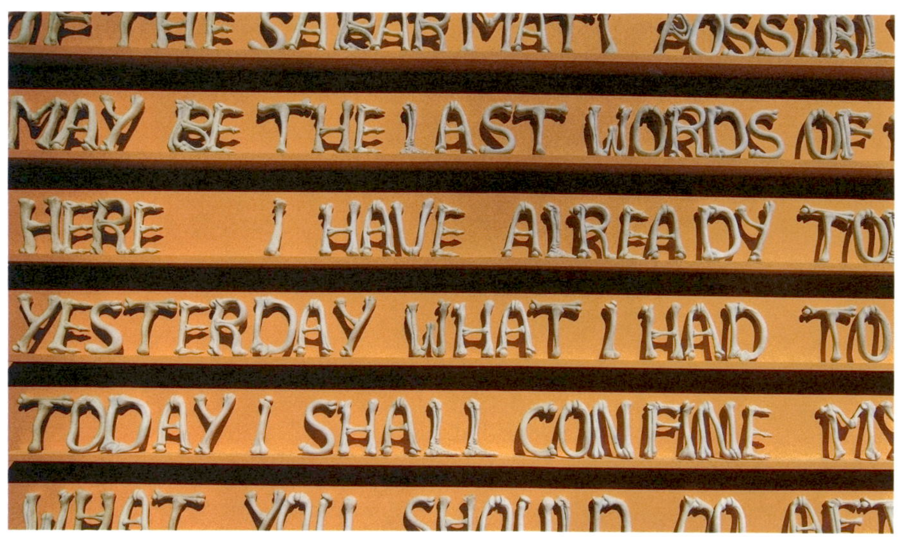

Figure 3
Jitish Kallat, *Public Notice 2*, 2007. Resin; 4,479 sculptural units; installation dimensions variable. The Saatchi Gallery, London.

Figure 4
Public Notice 2 (detail), 2007.

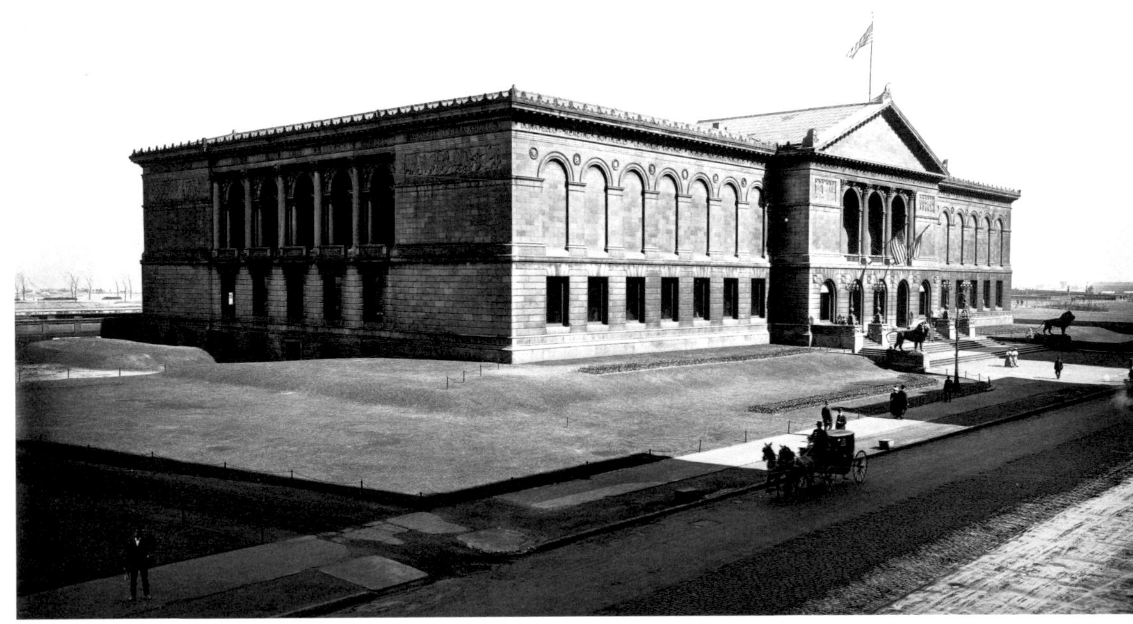

For the third work in this series, *Public Notice 3,* which opened at the Art Institute of Chicago on September 11, 2010, Kallat turned to another historically significant speech, that of Swami Vivekananda, who as a young, unknown Hindu monk delivered an important address about universal tolerance at the first World's Parliament of Religions at the Art Institute of Chicago on September 11, 1893.

SWAMI VIVEKANANDA IN CHICAGO

The World's Columbian Exposition of 1893 was held in Chicago to celebrate the four-hundredth anniversary of the discovery of the New World by Christopher Columbus and to announce to the world at large Chicago's reemergence from the devastation of the Great Fire of 1871. The World's Parliament of Religions was just one among a number of international meetings that were organized in conjunction with the exposition under the auspices of the World's Congress Auxiliary. Although the great fair itself was held on the South Side of Chicago on the lakefront in Jackson Park and stretched west along the Midway Plaisance to Washington Park, the assemblies that were part of the World's Congress Auxiliary were conducted in downtown Chicago. The site for these meetings was a newly completed Beaux–Arts style building on Michigan Avenue—designed by the Boston firm of Shepley, Rutan and Coolidge—that was to become, at the close of the World's Columbian Exposition, the new home of the Art Institute of Chicago (fig. 5).[9] Of all the meetings conducted here, the World's Parliament of Religions was by far the largest and most significant, taking place over seventeen days, September 11–27, 1893. Its sessions occupied two great temporary halls—named the Hall of Columbus and the Hall of Washington, each holding 3,000 people, with wooden seating throughout the main floor and in a wraparound gallery and a substantial stage for the speakers—that were constructed within the essentially U-shaped Art Institute building expressly for these large assemblages and that would be demolished immediately after the close of the fair (figs. 6–7). The space they occupied would over time be

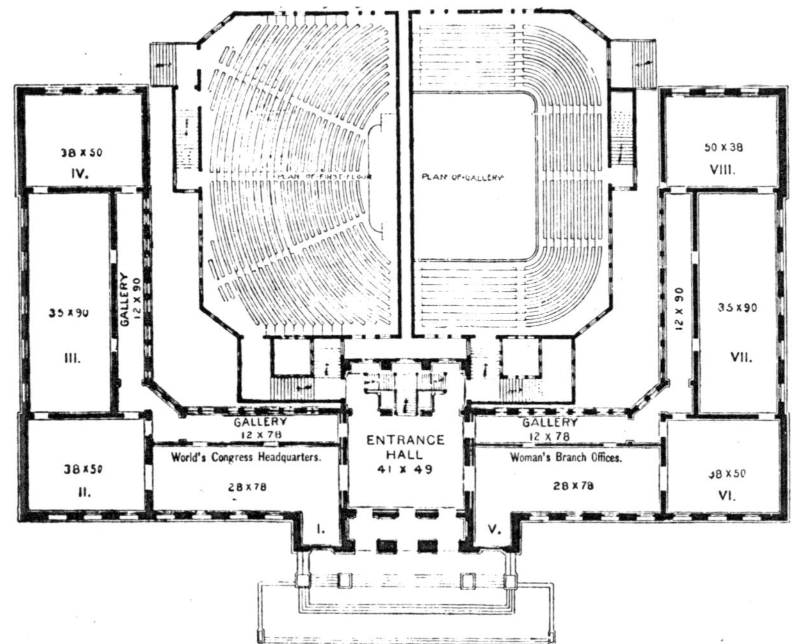

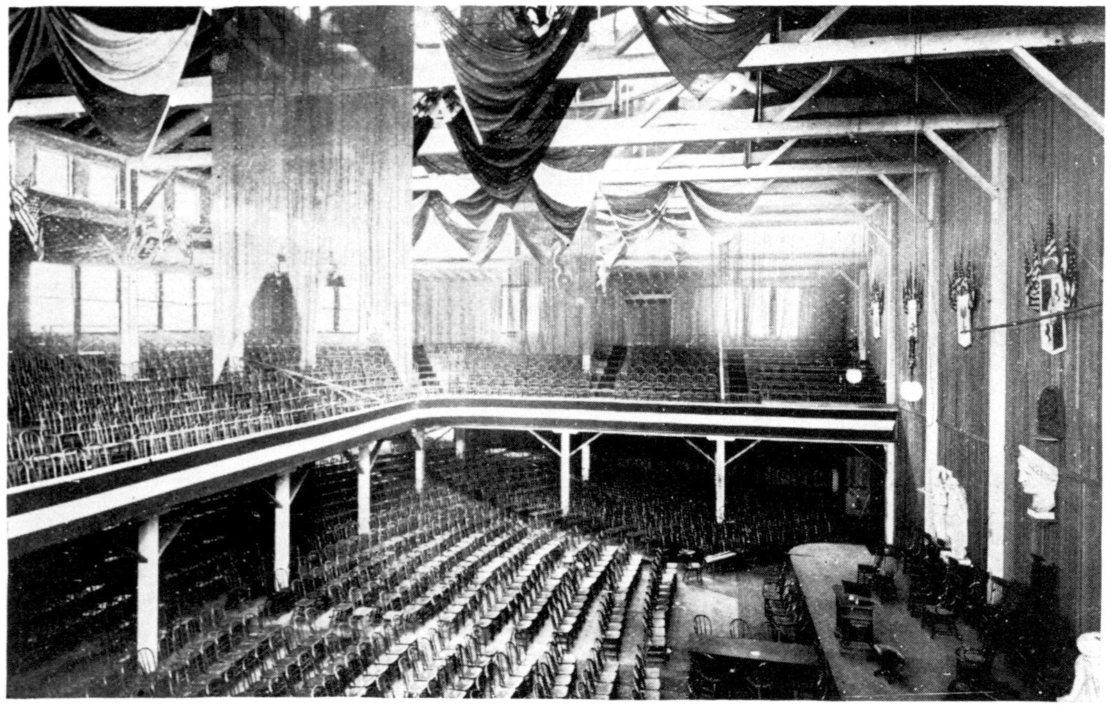

filled out with Fullerton Hall to the north (constructed in 1898) and the Ryerson Library to the south (completed in 1901), with the museum's Grand Staircase (not constructed until 1910) lying between them (fig. 8).[10]

At this venue among eminent religious scholars and representatives from all over the world, a young unknown monk from India, clad in a simple monastic robe and a turban, stole the show with his eloquence and created an awareness of Hinduism and its fundamental principles in the West for the very first time.

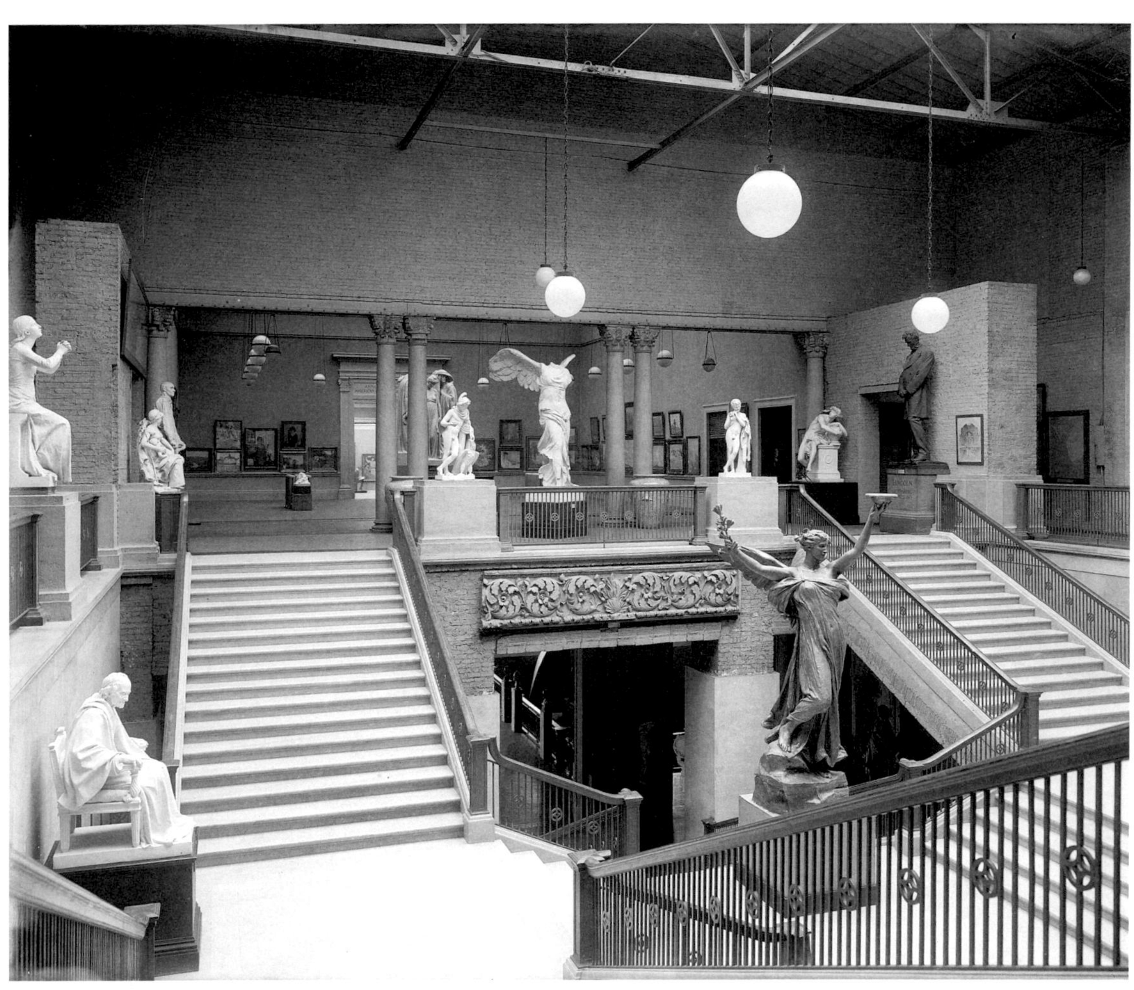

Figure 8
The Grand Staircase of the
Art Institute of Chicago,
constructed in 1910.

HISTORICAL BACKDROP

Swami Vivekananda was born Narendranath Datta on January 12, 1863, the son
of a lawyer in Calcutta (present-day Kolkata), then the capital of the British empire
in India. His spiritual quest took him to Ramakrishna Paramahamsa, a mystic
priest serving goddess Kali at the renowned Dakshineshwar temple on the outskirts
of Calcutta, whom he eventually accepted as his spiritual guru in 1885. Upon
Ramakrishna's death the following year, Vivekananda assumed leadership of his
disciples. He wandered the length and breadth of India as an itinerant monk, carrying just a staff and a waterpot, clad in an orange robe, the color that all of South
Asia regarded as the color of renunciation.[11] Vivekananda learned and preached
Advaita Vedanta philosophy: that all religions are true, and that service to man is
service to God.

While traveling around India, Vivekananda heard about the World's Parliament of
Religions that was being organized in Chicago, and with the help of funds raised by
his followers, including several Indian rulers, he left for the United States on May
31, 1893, assuming the monastic name Vivekananda (meaning "bliss of discerning
knowledge"). Arriving in July, he realized that he had no invitation to speak at the
parliament; but through several chance encounters he was introduced to Rev. John
Henry Barrows, a prominent Chicago Presbyterian minister and the President of the

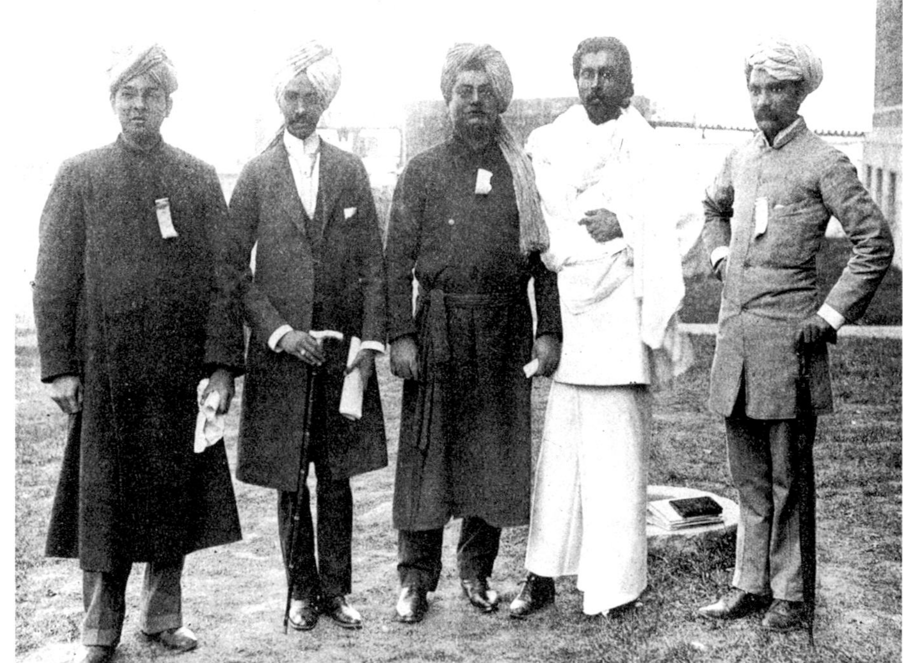

Figure 9
Swami Vivekananda (*center*) together with some of the other South Asian delegates to the 1893 World's Parliament of Religions, Chicago: *left to right*, Narasimhacharya, Lakshminarayan, H. Dharmapala, and Virchand Gandhi.

Parliament of Religions, who arranged for Vivekananda to attend as a representative of Hinduism (fig. 9). At the opening session in the Hall of Columbus on September 11, 1893, when Swami Vivekananda addressed the audience with the opening words, "Sisters and Brothers of America," there was a deafening ovation lasting full two minutes before he could continue with his speech, which addressed the universality of all faiths.[12] Vivekananda would later write in a letter: "The next day, all the papers announced that my speech was the hit of the day, and I became known to the whole of America."[13] Merwin-Marie Snell, secretary to Bishop John Keane of the Catholic University of America, was quoted as saying that "Swami Vivekananda . . . [was] beyond question the most popular and influential man in the Parliament."[14]

Vivekananda spoke several more times at the World's Parliament of Religions, and he was invited to speak at receptions, as well as in private homes, attracting widespread coverage in the press, and many followers. He spent the next couple of years lecturing in various places within the United States, teaching Vedanta and yoga, before traveling in Europe on his way back to India, all the while declining offers of teaching positions in the West. He received a triumphant welcome on his arrival in southern India in 1897. His inspiring speeches had a tremendous impact on Indian nationalist leaders including Mahatma Gandhi, Bal Gangadhar Tilak, and Subhash Chandra Bose. Vivekananda founded the Ramakrishna Mission in Calcutta on May 1, 1897, to propagate a vision to uplift the masses through educational and social work by the Ramakrishna order of monks. He traveled west once more, in 1899, during which time he founded the Vedanta societies in San Francisco and New York, and the Shanti Ashram in California. In 1900 he also attended the Congress of the History of Religions at the Sorbonne University in Paris in connection with the Exposition Universelle. Vivekananda passed away (took *samadhi*) on July 4, 1902, at the age of 39 at Belur Math near Calcutta, worn out by ill health and his hectic schedule.

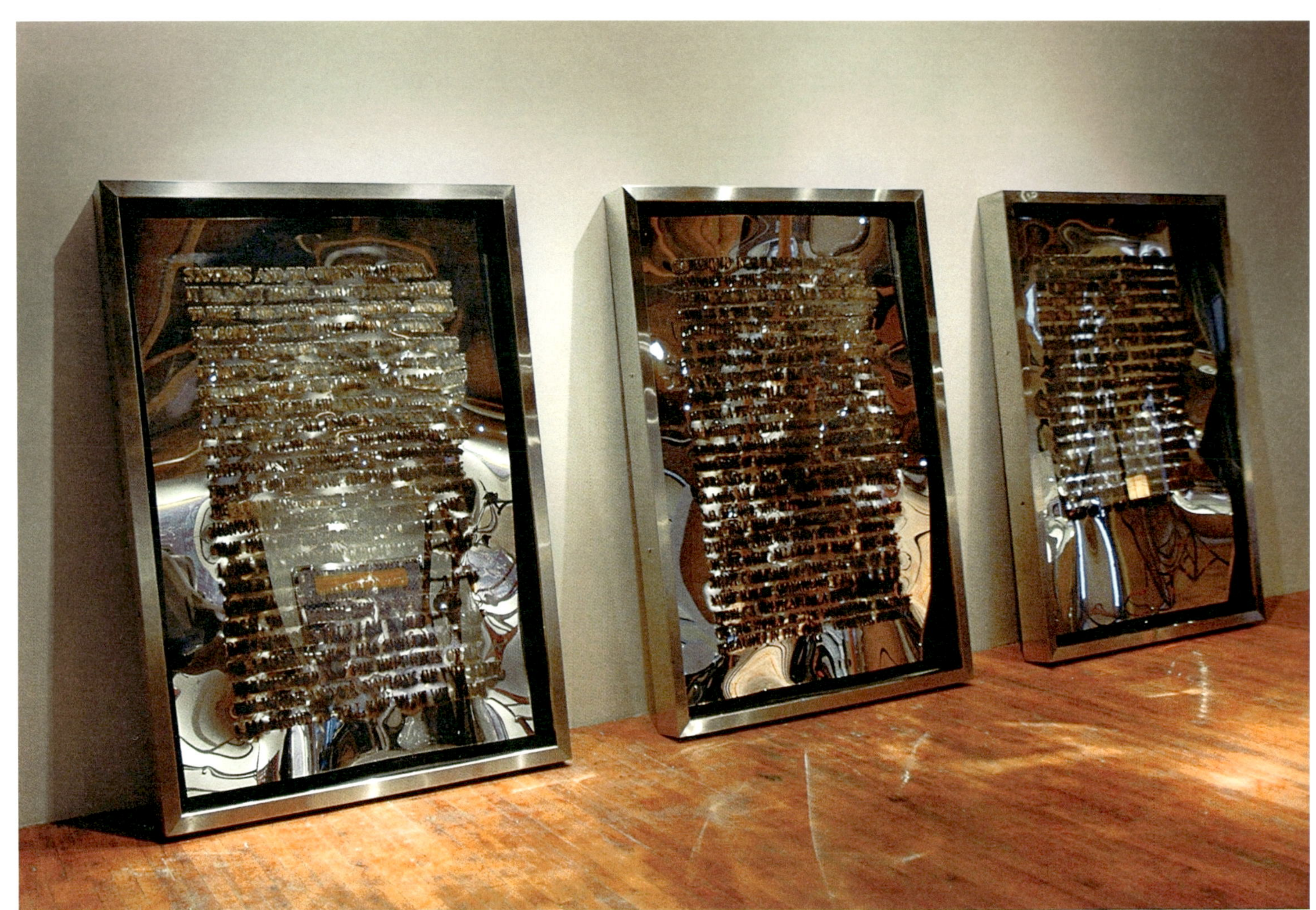

In addition to his introduction of the Vedanta branch of Hindu philosophy into America and Europe, Swami Vivekananda was influential in the revival of Hinduism in India in the late nineteenth and early twentieth centuries. By focusing on the ancient philosophic past of the Hindus, he was able to provide an alternative reformist view of Hinduism, which until then was viewed by India's colonial masters as a religion dominated by cult worship and "heathen" practices. Vivekananda was also the first to introduce yoga practices in the West. Most importantly, Vivekananda's teachings inspired an entire generation of Indian nationalist leaders and provided the moral fiber for the struggle to free India from the oppression of colonialism.

As a result of the efforts of the Indian American community not to let the memory of Swami Vivekananda be forgotten at the site of the Art Institute, a bronze commemorative plaque was installed on the centenary of his original address to the World's Parliament of Religions, on the north wall of the museum's Michigan Avenue lobby, just outside of Fullerton Hall, representing the space nearest to where Vivekananda had spoken. In addition, a portion of Michigan Avenue in front of the Art Institute was named "Honorary Swami Vivekananda Way" on November 11, 1995.[15]

Figure 10
Jitish Kallat, *Detergent*, 2004. Burned adhesive on acrylic mirror, wood; three panels, each 198.1 x 137.2 x 15.2 cm (78 x 54 x 6 in.). Collection of Vinita and Arun Agarwal, New York.

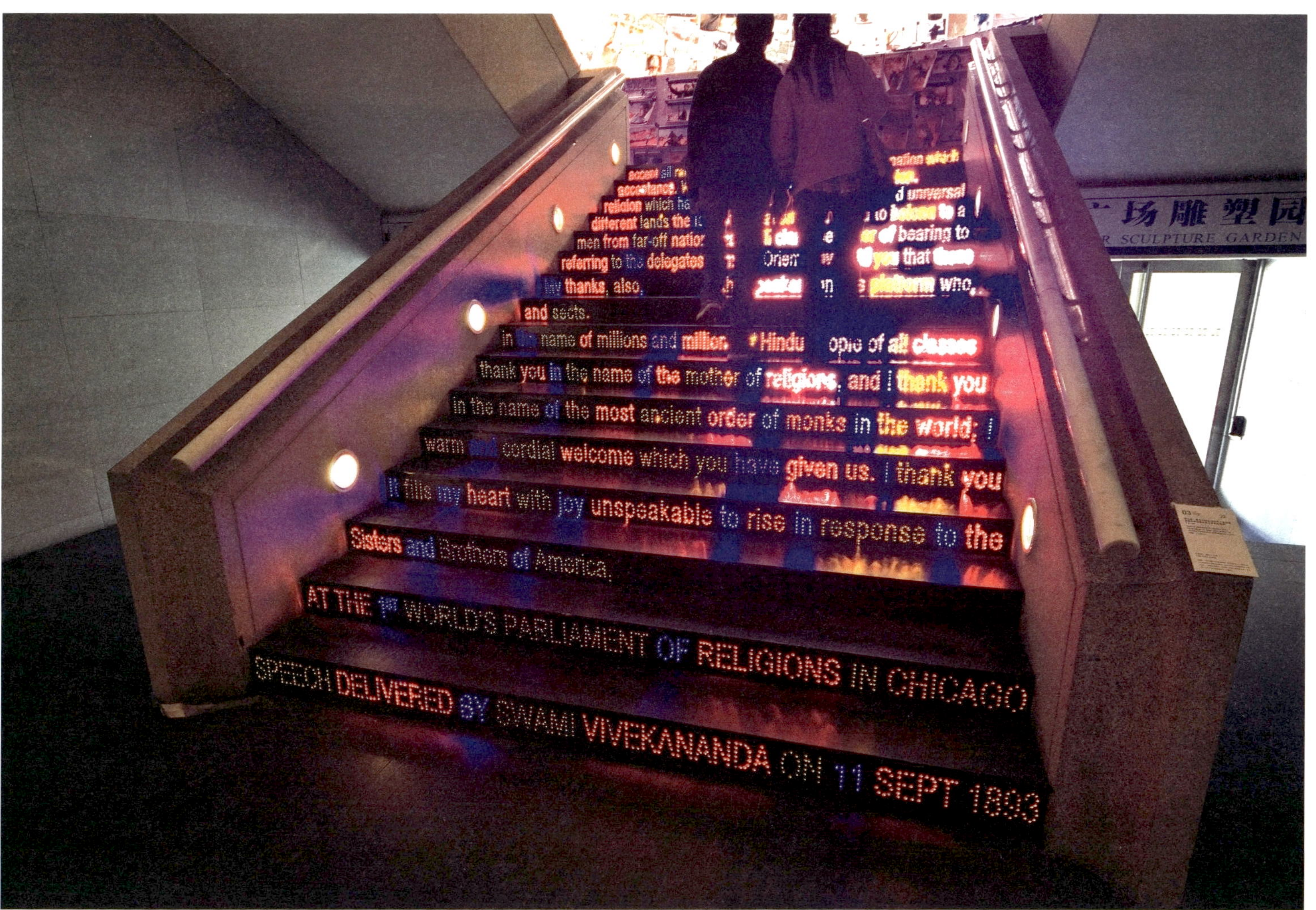

Figure 11
Jitish Kallat, *Detergent*, 2008. LED panels installed in the Guangdong Museum of Art, Guangzhou, China.

JITISH KALLAT AT THE ART INSTITUTE OF CHICAGO

In 2010 the contemporary artist Jitish Kallat was invited to present his site-specific light installation *Public Notice 3* at the Art Institute, inspired by Swami Vivekananda's famous speech of September 11, 1893. An earlier rendition of *Public Notice 3* can be seen in Kallat's triptych *Detergent* (2004), a text–based work in which Swami Vivekananda's speech was rendered—in the same fashion as the first *Public Notice*—in rubber adhesive and burned, or "cremated," onto acrylic mirrors (fig. 10), executed on the occasion of a solo exhibition entitled *The Lie of the Land* at the Walsh Gallery in Chicago (September 3–25, 2004).[16] When Kallat was initially invited to put together this exhibition, whose dates would straddle the third anniversary of the 2001 attacks on the World Trade Center and the Pentagon, he remembered another young Indian's journey to Chicago more than a century earlier, and created this work wherein the viewer's reflection gets distorted in the mirrored surfaces.[17]

19

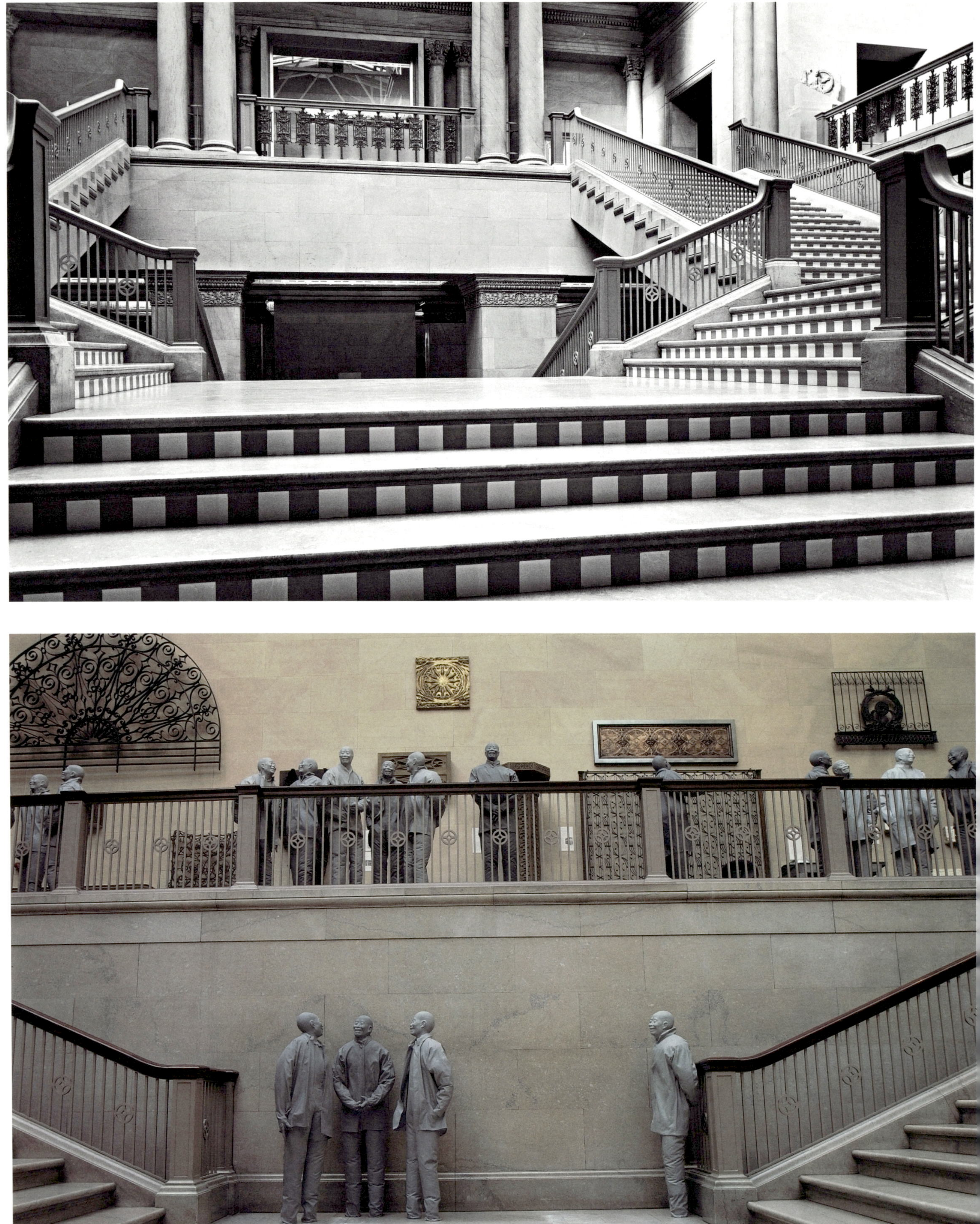

Kallat later reworked *Detergent* for the Guangzhou Triennial in China in 2008 at an exhibition entitled *Farewell to Post-Colonialism*. This time, the words of Swami Vivekananda from the 1893 Chicago address were spelled out in LED lights in the colors associated today with the terror codes instituted by the U.S. Department of Homeland Security, and were on the stairs of the Guangdong Museum of Art so that as visitors walked up and down the stairs they were constantly enveloped in the hues of the "terror" colors (fig. 11).

Finally, Kallat's *Detergent* came "home" when as *Public Notice 3* it opened on September 11, 2010, at the Art Institute of Chicago. Swami Vivekananda's evocative words calling for universal toleration and the end of bigotry and religious fanaticism were presented on the Woman's Board Grand Staircase, a space approximating the stages of the two temporary halls in which he originally spoke: the Hall of Columbus, where his opening address had been delivered; and the Hall of Washington—an area now largely occupied by the museum's Ryerson Library—where Vivekananda spoke on other occasions during the World's Parliament of Religions. The site-specific nature of this work in the very museum building that enshrines such memories invokes the spirit of the 1893 speech and juxtaposes it against the backdrop of the 9/11 attacks. Encountering it on the Grand Staircase and reading the words of Vivekananda in the process of climbing these stairs proved to be a moving experience for many museum visitors.

THE GRAND STAIRCASE AS AN ARTISTIC VENUE

Completed in 1910 and illuminated by a large skylight, the sole public staircase in the Art Institute's historic Michigan Avenue building has long been a hub of activity, a familiar meeting spot, and an immensely recognizable point of entry into the museum. In addition, it has naturally been the scene of countless events over the decades: receptions too numerous to mention, annual holiday concerts by Chicago-area high school choirs, and in 2007 performances by Yo-Yo Ma and the Silk Road Ensemble. Since 1987 the second-floor level surrounding the staircase has served as a gallery for the exhibition of decorative architectural elements in the permanent collection of the museum's Department of Architecture and Design, an installation entitled *Fragments of Chicago's Past*. The staircase and the gallery space encompassing it have also held sculptures by Cristoforo Stati and Gaston Lachaise, and most recently this spacious area has accommodated a massive brass chandelier from 1853 by the English architect and designer Augustus Welby Northmore Pugin.

But other artists have also chosen the Grand Staircase as a very public and very ambitious space for their installations as well. In 1977 conceptual artist Daniel Buren presented *Up and Down, In and Out, Step by Step, A Sculpture* on the Grand Staircase, enveloping its risers in stripes that also appeared on the outside steps fronting Michigan Avenue (fig. 12).[18] And in a major retrospective of his work organized by the Art Institute and the Hirshhorn Museum and Sculpture Garden, Spanish sculptor Juan Muñoz populated this spacious interior with dozens of his figurative pieces (fig. 13).[19]

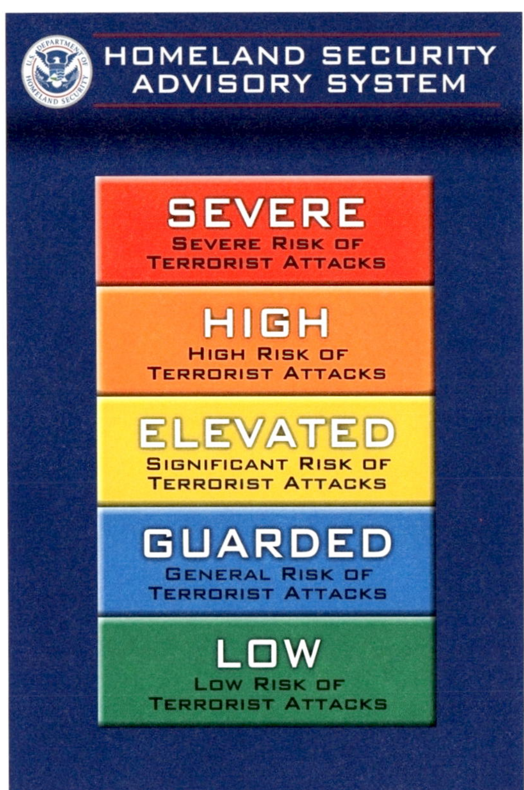

Figure 14
United States
Department of
Homeland Security
Advisory System,
introduced on
March 11, 2002.
In November 2010,
the department
announced plans to
replace this terrorism-
threat advisory system
with another program.

PUBLIC NOTICE 3

Text has played a significant role in Kallat's works, whether, for example, in the titles with which he labels his works, or in the oblique references to or wholesale adoption of the text of a significant speech, as he attempts to hold a mirror up to society.[20] For the presentation of *Public Notice 3*, the text of Vivekananda's speech is illuminated not in the seven colors of the spectrum, but in just five of them— red, orange, yellow, blue, and green—which were designated by the Department of Homeland Security Advisory System to signify different levels of security threats (fig. 14): green denotes "low" risk of terrorist attacks; blue indicates a "general" risk; yellow implies an "elevated" threat perception; orange, the color associated with religiosity in South Asia and the Himalayas, now stands for "high" threat, while red would mean that one is faced with a "severe" risk of a terrorist attack. Kallat is indignant at such co-opting of five of the colors from his paintbox.

Thus, Vivekananda's speech is presented on the risers of the Grand Staircase with 68,700 glowing LED (light–emitting diode) lights in the five colors of the threat codes in a font that was specially created for this work. A computer–generated program was used to distribute the application of the five colors randomly through-out the text. The speech begins on the lowest risers of the staircase and progresses upward, so that whichever path a visitor takes up the three flights, he or she will walk through the entire speech (fig. 15). The two lowest flights of stairs, which are east-facing and west-facing, eventually split into four as one ascends to the upper level. Likewise, the presentation of the final portion of Vivekananda's address is multiplied as well, almost as though it echoes in the space as it moves through the

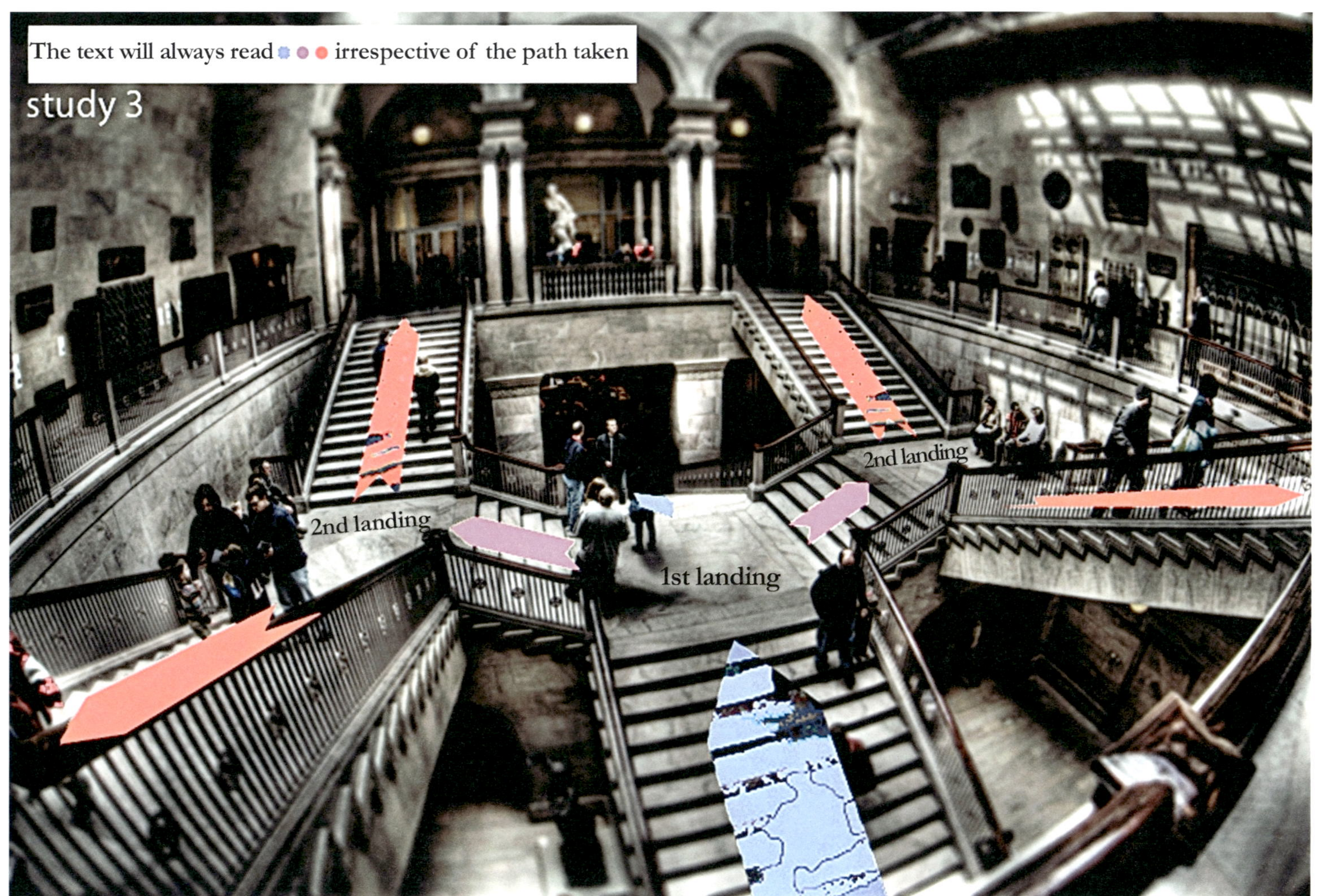

Figure 15
Jitish Kallat, preliminary design of *Public Notice 3*, May 2009, showing the sequencing of the text of Swami Vivekananda's speech up the flights of the Grand Staircase of the Art Institute of Chicago.

four cardinal directions—as one moves upwards, the skylight above creates a vision of the words spreading beyond this physical space, echoing into eternity.[21] The illumination of the text yields a subtle glow of the threat codes as one descends, and so it becomes not a passive commemoration but an active and contemplative space of transit and engagement.

In response to the public's reception of this site-specific piece, the Art Institute extended the installation of *Public Notice 3* to run through the tenth anniversary of the events of September 11, 2001. Jitish Kallat presented the work as a gift to the permanent collection of the Art Institute, where it constitutes the museum's first major gift of Indian contemporary art.

NOTES

1. Right-wing Hindu fundamentalists believe that the mosque had been constructed over the site of the birthplace of Rama, an incarnation of the god Vishnu. The demolition was the work of a mob armed with pickaxes and spades, violating a court order that had been issued to protect the site, and undertaken by a force so large that the police stood by helplessly. A recent verdict passed by the Lucknow Bench of the Allahabad High Court in September 2010 finally decided on the case after eighteen years. It is likely to be challenged in the Supreme Court by the Muslim community.

2. The artist Vivan Sundaram, for example, did an installation piece entitled *Memorial* (1993) in response to the sectarian riots between the Hindus and Muslims following the destruction of the Babri Mosque. Sundaram's work was inspired by the picture in a daily newspaper of a man lying dead on a burning street. For details, see Deeksha Nath, "Language of an Idealized Revolt: Sculptural Installation from the 1990s to the Present," in Gayatri Sinha (ed.), *Art and Visual Culture in India, 1857–2007* (Marg Publications, Mumbai, 2009), p. 252. For a summary, see Zehra Jumabhoy, "The Art of Politics," in *The Empire Strikes Back: Indian Art Today* (Saatchi Gallery, London, 2009), pp. 39–41. See Kallat's comments on these events in Sabine B. Vogel, "Strange and Familiar Images: Getting Acquainted with Contemporary Indian Art," in *Chalo! India: A New Era of Indian Art* (Prestel, 2009), p. 28.

3. For example, the feminist author Urvashi Butalia collected oral narratives of women into a true history of the partition and its consequences, in *The Other Side of Silence: Voices from the Partition of India* (Delhi, 1998).

4. For instance, in 1998 the artist Nalini Malini did an elaborate video installation entitled *Remembering Toba Tek Singh*, based on Sa'adat Hasan Manto's famous story, *Toba Tek Singh*, set at the time of the partitioning of India. In *Constructing the Memory of a Room* (2001–07), the artist Gargi Raina reconstructed the history of loss and partition by using domestic objects and images to revisit the memory of the loss of her ancestral home as a result of partition and migration from Pakistan to India. See Nath 2009 (note 2), pp. 257–58.

5. "The historical speech is a treasured document, a series of wise words which can become a template upon which to position today's world to see how the world has become misaligned"; Jitish Kallat in conversation with Shaheen Merali, in *Jitish Kallat: Public Notice 2*, edited by Shaheen Merali, exh. cat. (Bodhi Art, Singapore, 2008), p. 22.

6. It was exhibited at the 5th Asia–Pacific Triennial of Contemporary Art in the Queensland Art Gallery and Gallery of Modern Art, Brisbane, Australia. See Lynne Seear and Suhanya Raffel, eds., *The 5th Asia–Pacific Triennial of Contemporary Art,* exh. cat. (Brisbane, 2006).

7. Jitish Kallat, "Self Discovery," in Anupa Mehta, *India 20: Conversations with Contemporary Artists* (Mapin Publishing, Ahmedabad, 2007), pp. 112–13.

8. Jitish Kallat in conversation with Shaheen Merali (note 5).

9. The Art Institute of Chicago was founded as the Chicago Academy of Fine Arts and incorporated on May 24, 1879; it officially adopted the name of the Art Institute of Chicago in 1882. The institution had been housed in various leased spaces before buying a building on South Michigan Avenue at Van Buren Street. It later demolished that structure and erected a new one on the same site in 1887. The Art Institute's present Beaux-Arts style building on Michigan Avenue at Adams Street was planned in cooperation with the World's Columbian Exposition on land set aside by the Chicago Park District. This building was occupied by the World's Congress Auxiliary from May 1 through October 31, 1893, after which the Art Institute took possession of the building. See Linda S. Phipps, "The 1893 Art Institute Building and the 'Paris of America': Aspirations of Patrons and Architects in Late Nineteenth–Century Chicago," in *The Architecture of the Art Institute of Chicago*, a special issue of *The Art Institute of Chicago Museum Studies* 14, 1 (1988), pp. 30–31.

10. See Jane H. Clarke, "The Art Institute's Guardian Lions," in *The Architecture of the Art Institute of Chicago*, a special issue of *The Art Institute of Chicago Museum Studies* 14, 1 (1988), pp. 102–03 n. 3.

11. Ironically, this color has become associated in our public memory with Code Orange, a high level of terror threat according to the codes issued by the U.S. Department of Homeland Security following the tragic events of 9/11—a chain of events that is at the center of the Kallat's *Public Notice 3*.

12. Walter R. Houghton, ed., *Neely's History of the Parliament of Religions and Religious Congresses at the World Columbian Exposition* (Chicago, 1893), p. 64.

13. Vivekananda, quoted in Swami Chetanananda, *Vivekananda: East Meets West; A Pictorial Biography* (Vedanta Society of St. Louis, 1995), p. 59.

14. *Indian Mirror*, March 9, 1894, quoted in Marie Louise Burke, *Swami Vivekananda in the West: New Discoveries* (Advaita Ashram, Calcutta, 1983), p. 85; see Chetanananda (note 13), p. 59.

15. The City Council of Chicago passed a resolution to that effect on October 2, 1995. The Indian American community also erected a bronze statue (over ten feet high and weighing approximately 1,000 kg) outside the Hindu Temple of Greater Chicago at Lemont, Illinois, on a mound that has been named Vivekananda Hill. It was unveiled to the community on July 12, 1998.

16. See *Jitish Kallat: Chicago, Mumbai; The Lie of the Land, Humiliation Tax,* exh. cat. (Walsh Gallery, Chicago/ Gallery Chemould, Mumbai, 2004).

17. Kallat was struck by the coincidence of dates of Vivekananda's speech and the terrorist attacks in the U.S. and the fact that 108 years separated these two events: "The figure 108 . . . is regarded as sacred in Hindu numerology"; Kallat in conversation with Shaheen Merali (note 5), p. 26.

18. See Anne Rorimer, "*Up and Down, In and Out, Step by Step, A Sculpture*, a Work by Daniel Buren," *The Art Institute of Chicago Museum Studies* 11, 2 (Spring 1985), pp. 140–155.

19. See Neal Benezra et al., *Juan Muñoz*, exh. cat. (Hirshhorn Museum and Sculpture Garden, Smithsonian Institution, Washington, D.C./The Art Institute of Chicago, 2001), pp. 134–37, 143.

20. Jitish Kallat in conversation with Nina Miall, in *Jitish Kallat: Universal Recipient,* exh. cat. (Haunch of Venison, London, 2008), p. 56. See also Gina Fairley, "Navigating Contemporary India," *Asian Art News* 19, 3 (2009), p. 94.

21. Original plans for the Grand Staircase envisaged an elaborately decorated dome that was never constructed due to the lack of funds. See Phipps (note 9), pp. 43–44.

It has often been said that the nineteenth century was besmirched by colonial expansion, creating a legacy of shame that was inherited by Western Europe. Subsequently, the twentieth century was dominated by the might of North America and its ultimate position as the sole, surviving superpower. Within the realm of current probabilities, it seems that the twenty-first century will be marked by the supremacy of Asia, specifically China and India, the current leading engines of recovery in a time of widespread economic malaise.

Recent art history, perhaps owing to its supposed love affair with postmodernity, has gradually enforced an expansion, extending and incorporating a partially globalized playing field and allowing a new internationalism to slowly emerge. Still in the process of formation, with an infrastructure in its infancy, this sense of internationalism is entirely dependent on an expansion in the art market and the gaining of new tastes to formulate a fitting agency. Such an undertaking prompts a much-needed escape from the traditional, guarded domain of the arts as this starts to haphazardly reflect itself in its inclusionary and pluralistic vision—a vision that some have termed "global arts" and others as "world arts." Whichever term one uses to describe this slow metamorphosis, it remains a vision tempered and grossly affected by existing conditions, most especially an uneven, uninterested art world with an encoded Eurocentric history. Subverting this quotidian is a challenging prospect, specifically if one were to consider the resources necessary to undo the ruling and narrow mindset of its policed principles.

As the poet Mina Loy once suggested, "The flux of life is pouring its aesthetic aspect into your eyes, your ears—and you ignore it because you are looking for your canons of beauty in some sort of frame or glass case or tradition."[1]

The last two decades of the twentieth century have proved somewhat unique; a thirst for change has emerged, providing the unique prospect of framing Asia through its economic impact, leading eventually to a new market for these interpretations. The convergence of this condition has become a subject matter for a number of contemporary makers and thinkers, providing a sustainable balancing act for their desire to record its accelerated urbanization. It appropriately renders their evaluations and imaginations within the postmodern challenges of active subjectivities, resolved by the complexities, experiments, and impact of emerging media and technologies. The current fervor for artworks that have emerged from Asia can be traced to the strong "leap forward" of these works. Known as the Chinese Avant-Garde, this group in the late 1980s included Ai Weiwei, Yang Fudong, Song Dong, and later, Cao Fei, among numerous others. This movement followed on the successful heels of the Fifth Generation of Chinese filmmakers, those who were celebrated at the Cannes and Venice festivals in the mid-eighties for their exalted technical craft; their brave, if not caustic, narratives; and their vision of the moral quagmire of the Cultural Revolution.

The first decade of the twenty-first century saw a similar wave of success stories emerging from the Indian subcontinent, albeit one on a smaller scale and one that held sway for a shorter period of time. The same meteoric rise and downfall in gallery spaces—with artworks from artists' studios arriving relatively fresh at auction houses—resulted in their treading the boards of the Basel international art fair with its assortment of financially driven collectors, which included a bevy of short-term investors and art-fund managers. The rise of the arts market, a new phenomenon for India, started to both create and affect the visibility of the arts in neighboring countries, with a galley of artists from Pakistan, Thailand, and further west, Iran and Lebanon visibly framed within the burgeoning contemporary Asian fold.

This scenario lasted for a short period, compared to the wave of interest in the Chinese Avant-Garde, and the whole movement was quickly abandoned with the global collapse of banks and mortgage companies, affected by the subprime-mortgage debacle arising in the United States. The hasty demise of the momentarily meteoric Indian art market can be further traced to the overpricing of such young artists from a fresh market, especially when combined with the desire to provide a sufficient number of works in a fashion that left behind the notion of unique pieces, in exchange for the blustery serialization of some artists' works.

In this second decade of our new millennium, where the hard times still continue, much that seemed to be part of the contemporary art scene has disappeared, including prestigious and flamboyant galleries, fast-paced curators, questionable studio practices, and the anxieties of pacing collectors. What remains are the interesting and strengthened cohorts that have survived from the two previous decades, now recognized as an era of bust and boom.

The practice of the artist Jitish Kallat survives, having blossomed during times of duress as well as during the highs of these past two complex decades, demonstrating a strength that has transformed his works from an earlier practice based on the production of paintings to one that is increasingly accompanied by large-scale and ambitious sculptures (see fig. 9), lens-based installations (see fig. 11), and recent video works. One victim of his success is the virtual loss of his own skilled and fluid writing on contemporary art from India and its fascinating relationship to the city—but what has been lost to the printed word has been progressively gained in his visualizations of a world held in a brace position.

THE EARLY YEARS

While Jitish Kallat was born in Mumbai, his cultural heritage is that of Kerala, a coastal state in the southern aspect of the Indian subcontinent. Kerala is known for its long history, dedicated to communist and socialist ideals that have given it a unique set of characteristics. It holds the literacy record for the country, which, at approximately 92%, has made this region the forerunner of policies related to the development and progression of secular rights following India's independence in 1947. The state has been at the forefront in guarding its multifaith communities and securing rights for those disadvantaged by the persistence of such archaic systems as the caste and class system.

Kerala's lavish landscape—rich in spices and, more recently, the setting for tourist ventures—has provided the manpower for the middle-management structure of the development projects in the nearby Gulf States. The Indian state has quietly become a unique hub and microenvironment for knowledge gained from such worldly experience and intercultural contact.

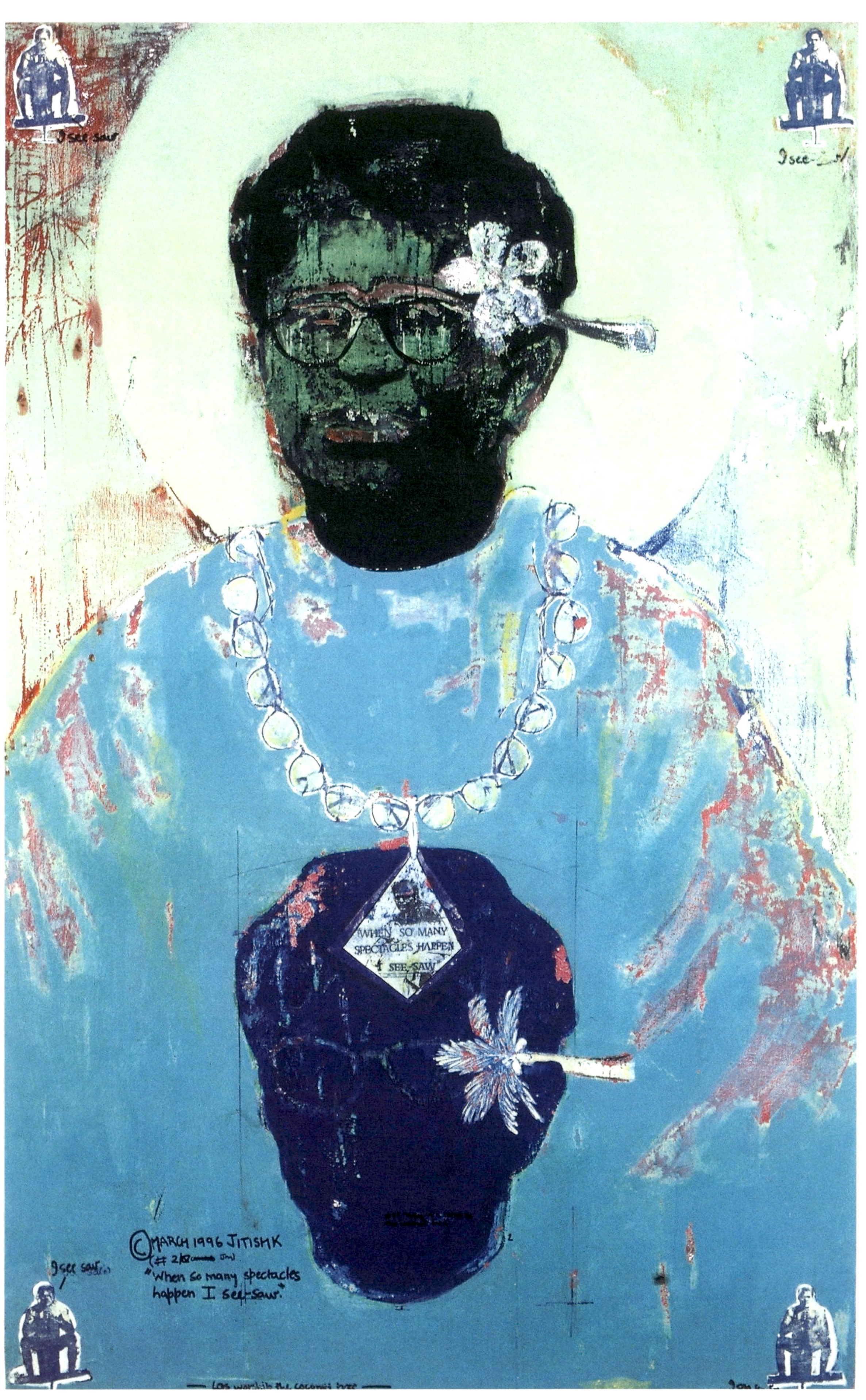

Figure 1
Jitish Kallat, *When So Many Spectacles Happen I See-Saw*, 1995. Mixed media on canvas; 152.4 x 96.5 cm (60 x 38 in.). Private collection.

The current group of successful contemporary artists from India are more than well represented by individuals from this state—and here I would include N. N. Rimzon, Surendran Nair, T. V. Santhosh, and Riyas Komu. Like Kallat, the mainstay of their subject matter rises out of personal concern and a deep sense of responsibility. Often they engage subjects affected by the turn of the millennium, whether this may mean the political and economic plights of the individual, or afflicted societies caught in the concomitant age of terror.

Kallat's early work reflected many of these concerns, which have been consistently mined in the ensuing years. One such area has been the need to express and "demute" the voice of the subaltern, a term that refers to persons who socially, politically, and geographically remain outside a society's hegemonic power structure. Kallat resolved his heartfelt concern in simultaneously folding their place into the minuscule and plethoric sweeps of urban India. His own family moved from Kerala to Mumbai in the 1950s, when the city, known then as Bombay, was itself being reimagined and recast within the growing success of Indian cinema, creating a genre known now as Bollywood. Mumbai was becoming the main subject of cinematic voices and a background for stories, glories, and morbidities: this dark and dangerous hinterland held romantic and melodic influences on generations to come. Kallat, like thousands of others, realized the potential of stories to be told from this vast metropolis. Mumbai's accumulated impossibilities, with its shifting tides of desire, demonstrated a scale beyond historical precedence or imagination. Mumbai/Bombay had became an uncharted subject since its colonial heydays, its underground networks of piracy and brotherhood a new shared space beyond the familial and far from the rise of its economic might, an empire city with and without rules, a place beyond time and of very few gaps. As Kabir, the great mystic poet of the fifteenth century, once wrote:

> In that place there is no happiness or unhappiness,
> No truth or untruth,
> Neither sin nor virtue.
> There is no day or night, no moon or sun,
> There is radiance without light.[2]

Enrolling in the prestigious Sir J. J. School of Art—which had produced the great artists of the preceding modern period including V. S. Gaitonde, Tyeb Mehta, S. H. Raza, and F. N. Souza—Kallat would have found himself arriving in a sacred space, dedicated to refining ideas and procuring a perch from which to speak and give voice to that within. The earlier works, all paintings, were guided by, if not dedicated to, a sense of surveillance of his new surroundings and of finding a mode of address, illustrating an urban tempo of voices that needed to be heard. This "demuting" had started to successfully provide an innovative use of textures and scale, incorporating the vast body of the subaltern's twisted realities and taciturn fright. The painting *When So Many Spectacles Happen I See-Saw* (1995; fig. 1) provides a prime example of the complexity of his task and the means by which the use of the street is increasingly marked in graphics that quote posters, notices, and billboards that rally the cries for justice and equality. The painting has a scraped surface, a practice that Kallat held onto in the following years, as a way to investigate a sense of defacement and enforced removal in his works. The main figure's face is painted in a dark hue—one often used for the depiction of the poisoned but surviving power of Shiva, the god of destruction and sustenance, the third aspect of the Hindu pantheon. The face becomes replicated underneath, in a double-portrait that quirkily provides an afterimage. These inventive tropes of surfaces and hues and mechanisms of seeing and looking are playful as well as troubled. Alongside other works of the same caliber, a portfolio of caustic renditions is attributed to a political degeneracy that Kallat feels is ready for exploration. One aspect, which can be traced through many further renditions as inflammatory repositories of a set of dormant references, appears as that which Kallat calls an "inner mythology."

A STEEP RISE

The recurring, even repetitious concerns of many in Kallat's generation find an uncanny ease in communicating within a burgeoning visual culture that starts to reek of threats and instability within the economic boom and bust and the ensuing upheavals. The new, fresh anxieties created a period of stagnation in the secular progress of the heaving mass of an uprooted India and its elevated position within Asia. The world, it seems, has started to create its own coded cultural production, often reflected in Indie films, immobilizing post-Rushdie novels, and more relevantly here, in the growingly politicized fine art renditions of Kallat and his cohorts. T. V. Santhosh uses solarized images from media sources, Subodh Gupta makes monumental sculptures out of domestic vessels—even to the scale of depicting the mushroom cloud of Hiroshima—and Kallat surveys threatened subjects, tight smiles against paranoid backgrounds of flanked horizons and neon skies.

Figure 2
Jitish Kallat, *Italics (War Dance)*, 2002. Mixed media on canvas; 228.6 x 152.4 cm (90 x 60 in.). Private collection.

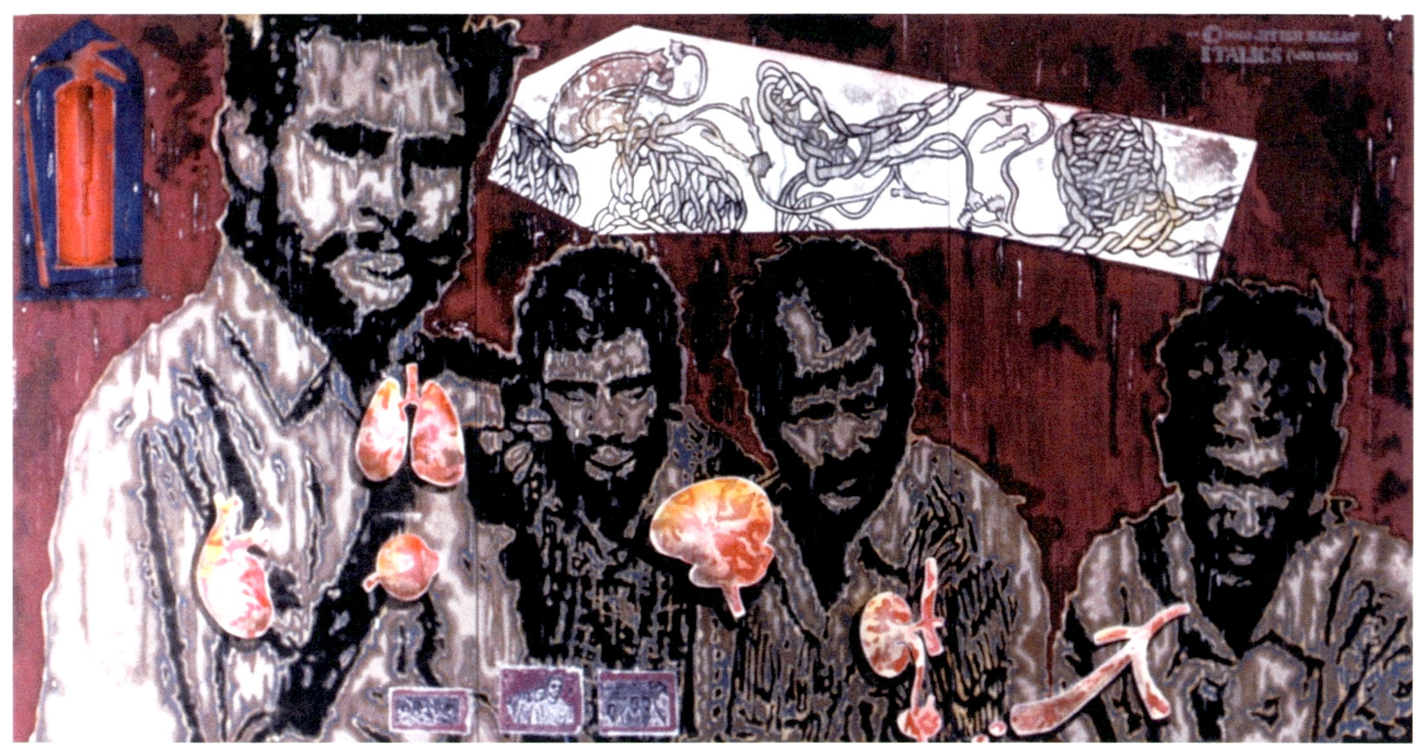

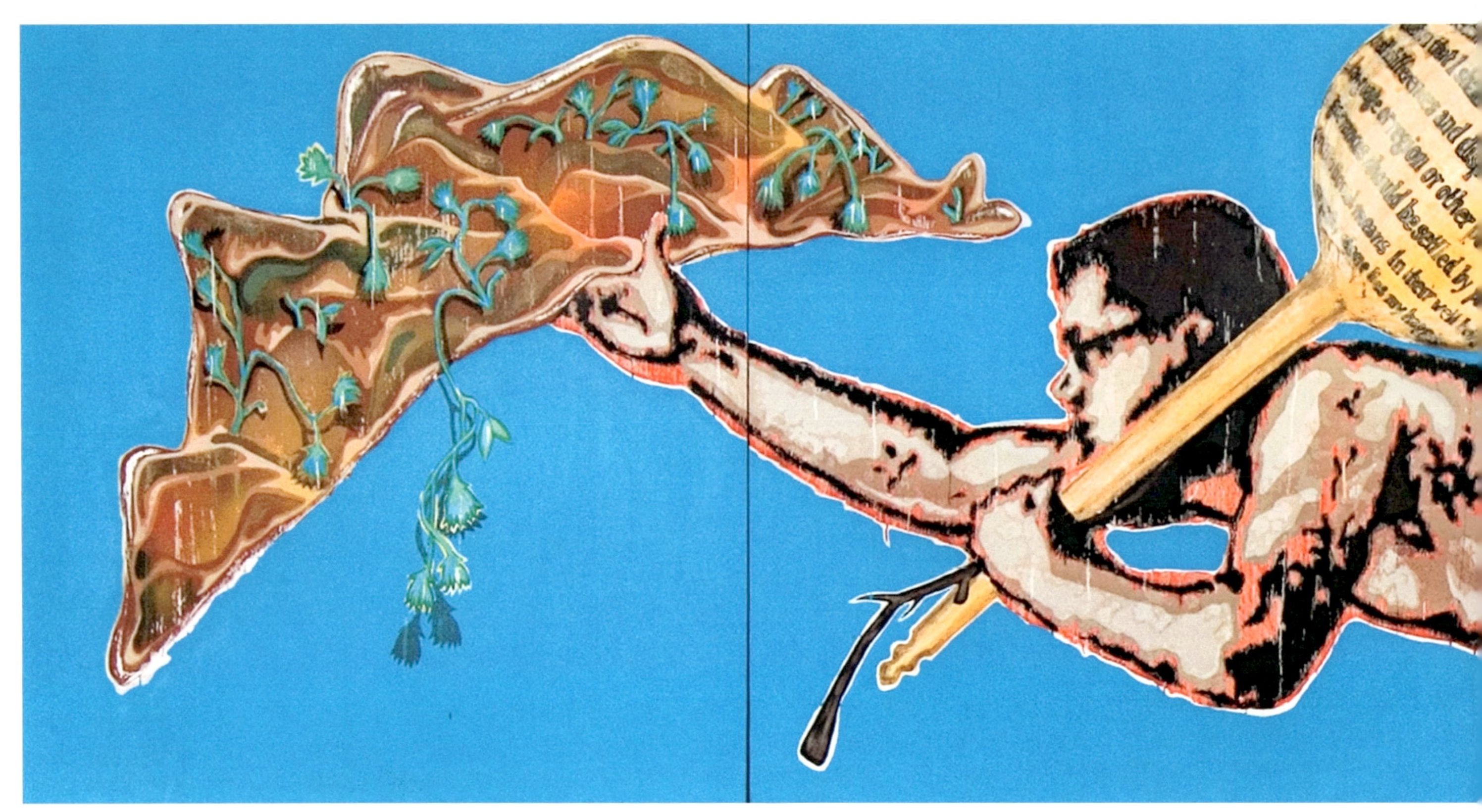

This generation of artists quickly came to the fore in the late 1990s and became recognizable names in the early cultural mapping of the new millennium: a generation that came to be known as the Contemporary Indian artists, a vox populi label that revealed a classification apart from the previous generation of modernists. Referring to terms such as "modern" and "contemporary" Indian art as "simplistic user-friendly categories" created by auction houses, Kallat explains in a recent interview: "Historians are more nuanced in their approach. The works of the Indian modernists need urgent re-evaluation. Interestingly, if we look at the works some of these artists were making in the decade following Indian Independence, one can spot traces of a subterranean narration about the nation—the agrarian hope or the urban dream. While the figure registered on the canvas might reference European modernism or employ the techniques of cubism, the theme of nationalism or nation-building that emerges through their practice has a logic that will align it with the postmodern. A re-evaluation will make us realize that their practice was far more complex than it appears."[3]

The advent of such a dichotomous art scene, instigated by the economic power of the market, has created a curatorial, second history of contemporary Indian art, which remains, at the moment, divided between that which gained its visibility prior to the nineties and that which emerged from its partial eclipse and experienced increasing disdain. The subject matter in Kallat's work, I would argue, is also represented in his generation of artists and remains infused with concerns similar to those found in the work of his predecessors; issues that are firm in the belief that the traditional subject and role of painting and sculpture can be aligned to

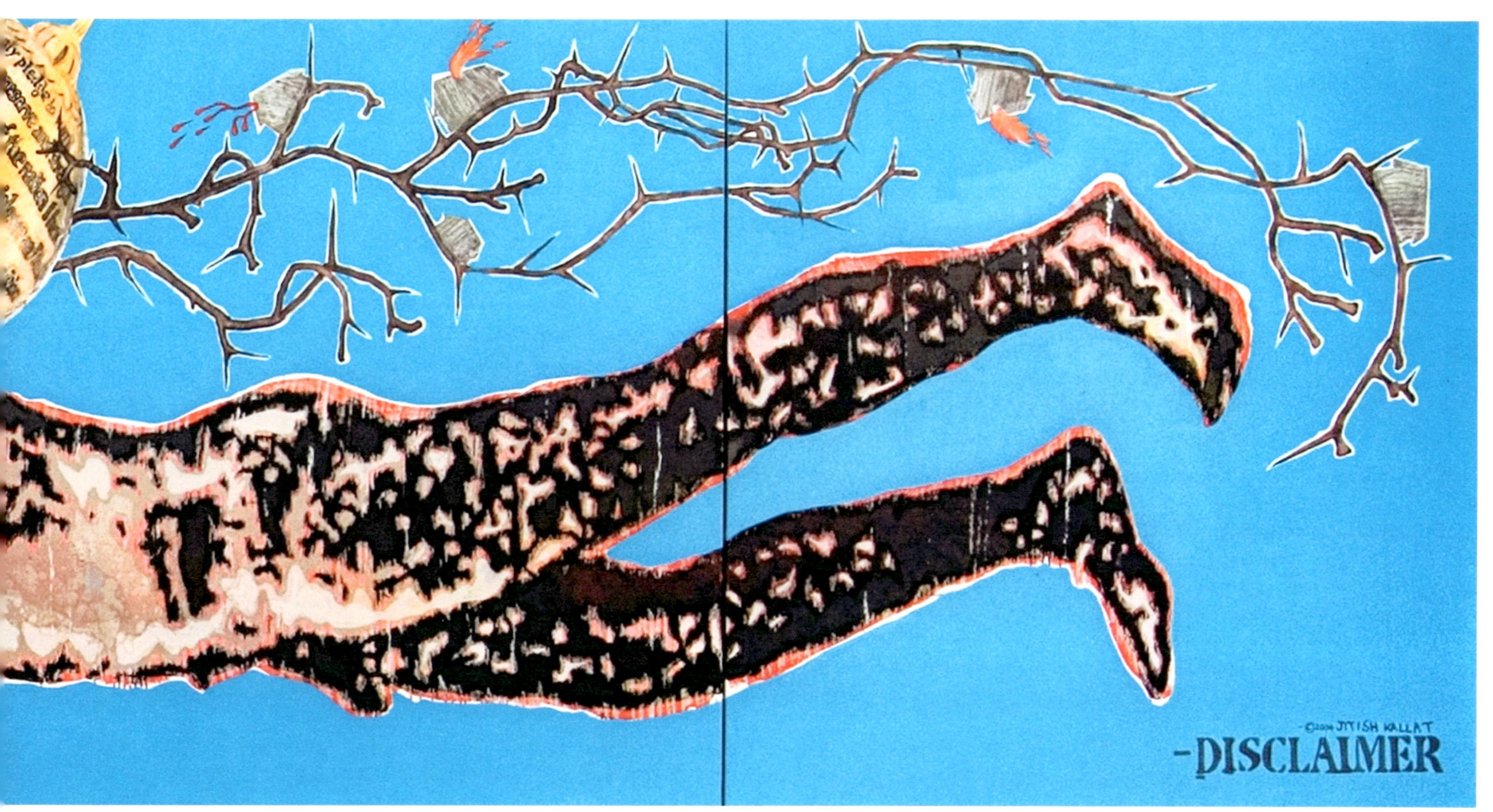

the political agency of *functional transformation* (*Umfunktionierung*), a Brechtian notion that conveys that the artistic position of intellectuals and artists should not merely "be that of supply in the production process but, rather, should attempt to transform it, along the lines of existing political struggle."[4] The "subterranean narration about the nation—the agrarian hope or the urban dream" that Kallat described above is one of the ways to compare his work to the rigorous attempts by Bhupen Khakhar to imbue his compositions with street scenes, and it enables us to see how Kallat could explore, in minute detail, the magnetic vitality of the street and its economic viability as panoramically captured in *Artist Making Local Call* (2005; see pp. 82-83). The semi-aerial paintings of towns and locales by Gulam Sheikh in the early 1970s and 1980s can also be used as a point of comparison with Kallat. It seems that these very subjects are further evaluated in the portraits that he began to define in the nineties, of young men whose lives are defined by the battle to survive and scrape together a living in cities that were becoming over-stretched by a population explosion created by the constant drift of urban-bound rural communities.

"The profound and interesting development one finds in the artist's oeuvre is his take on the tradition of portraiture. The subject is a constant transmutation of the subordinated, the focus consequently on the state of economic excitement in the tenacious condition of urban acclimatization. This theme, which has been consistently evaluated and strongly addressed by Kallat, is evident in his earlier paintings, including *Italics (War Dance)* (2002; fig. 2) and *Disclaimer* (2004; fig. 3), in

Figure 3
Jitish Kallat,
Disclaimer, 2004.
Mixed media on
canvas; 175.3 x
731.5 (69 x 288 in.).
Collection of
The Guild, Mumbai.

33

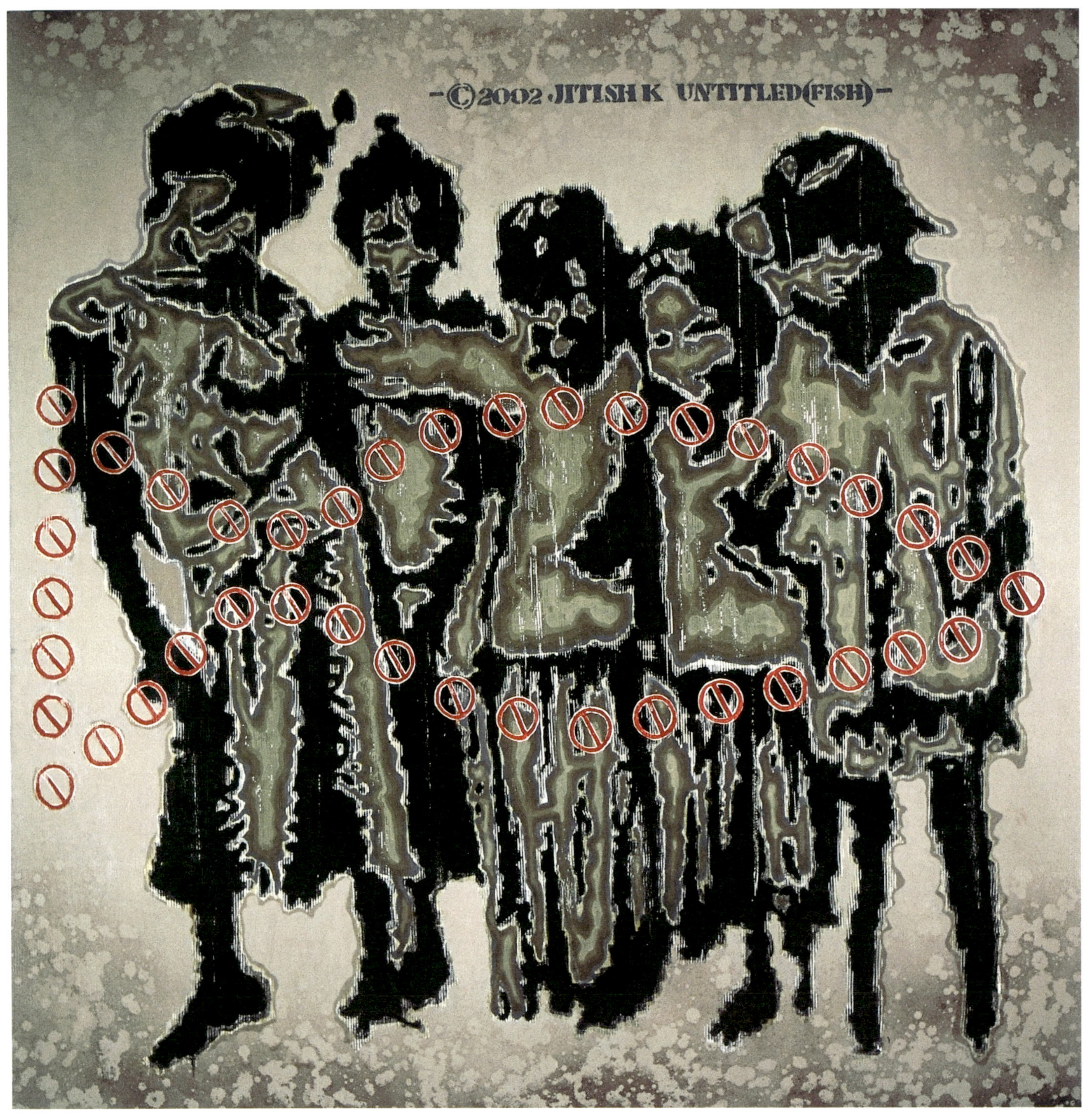

Figure 4
Jitish Kallat, *Untitled (Fish)*, 2002. Mixed media on canvas; 175.3 x 175.3 cm (69 x 69 in.). Private collection.

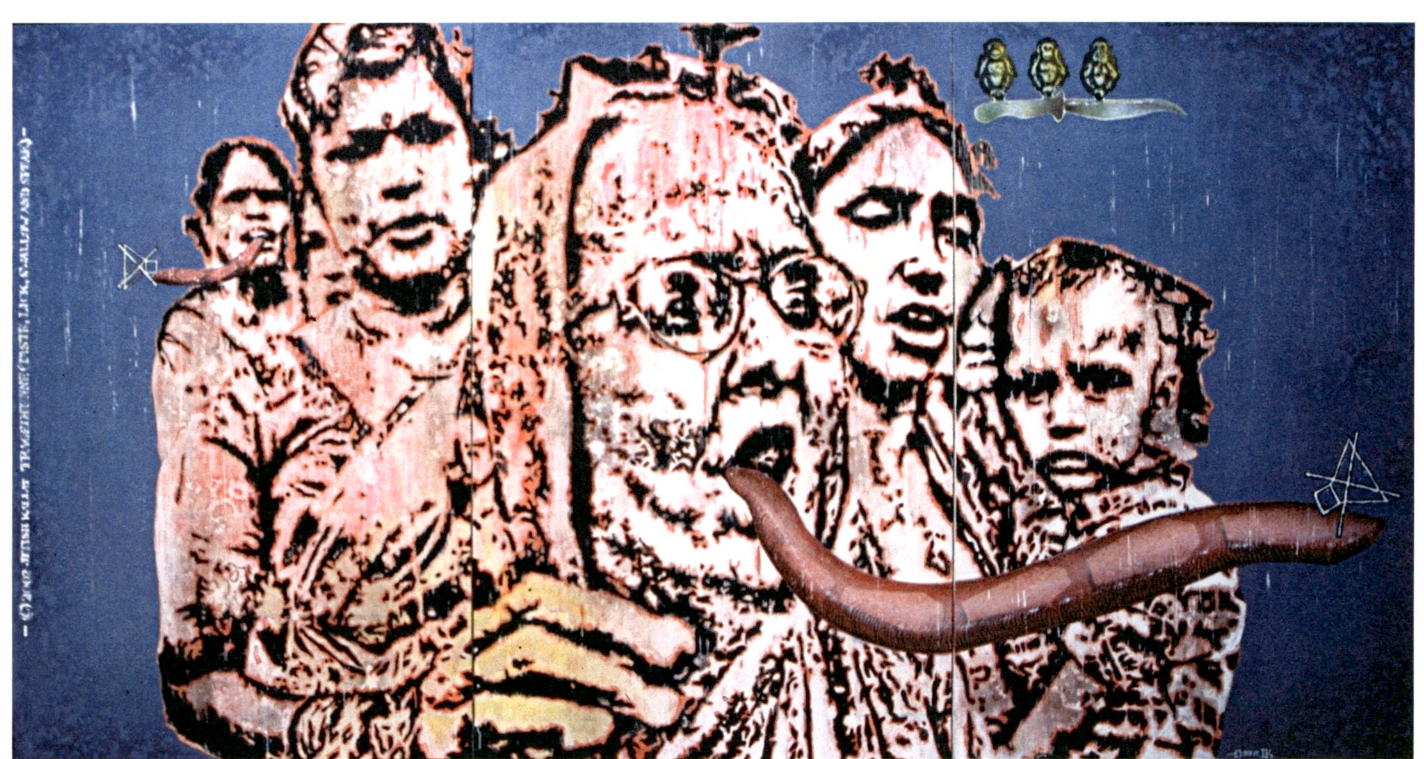

which a pattern starts to manifest itself in the proclivity of the suburban subaltern, the constituted reality that is seen and heard by others as well as by ourselves, but never before so dramatically rendered.

Kallat's overt use of collage to construct these large canvases permits a distortion of space. The portraits were initially placed against a color field, later replaced by a vertical striped background reminiscent of canvas tents and awnings used at tea parties and other such ceremonies: a design effectively Victorian, but with the usual green-and-white stripes replaced by a vibrant mixture of violets, pinks, and blues. These portraits, derived from photographs that the artist takes of guards outside the burgeoning gated communities of middle-class Mumbai suburbs, start to represent a paradox of individuated mass, with specific features and characteristics but in a hegemonic horde. These large-scale works overtly reference photocopying and cut-and-paste methodologies and technologies that permit incremental upscaling of low-resolution images. This incremental upscaling and ambivalence enables Kallat to articulate the manifest incremental increase in the local suburban use of low-class labor, the management of power and fear, and the subsequent rise in the security industry as a necessary precondition for livability."[5]

Untitled (Fish) (2002; fig. 4) is another example of Kallat's distilled emotive use of the subaltern mass: here Kallat tries to address the exploding mass of bodies (on the streets) that occupy every niche and space in Mumbai's condensation. This gray composition of a group of young children imparts yet another shadowy world of outlines and "knot-bodies" filled with an internal fuzz—of what could be visually deemed to represent an unrequited ambition, a buzz of energy, of life itself, formed and yet formless, quizzically looking back from the overcast world of the unidenti-fied. The horizons, the rainbow colors, the recurring messages from Kallat's imagi-

Figure 5
Jitish Kallat, *Tragedienne (Taste, Lick, Swallow and Speak)*, 2002. Mixed media on canvas; 228.6 x 457.2 cm (90 x 180 in.). Collection of Gazala Bagash, Dubai.

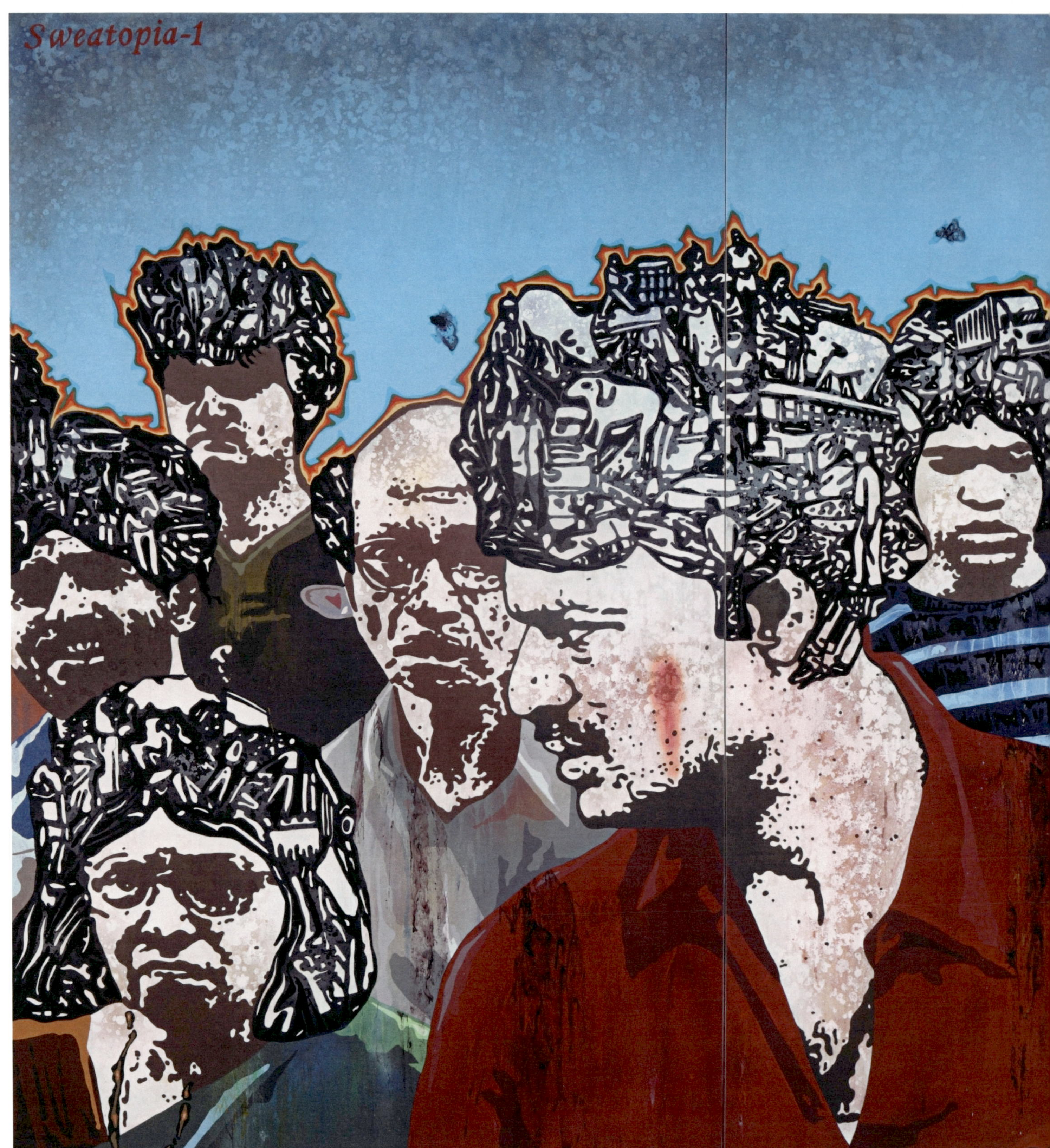
Sweatopia-1

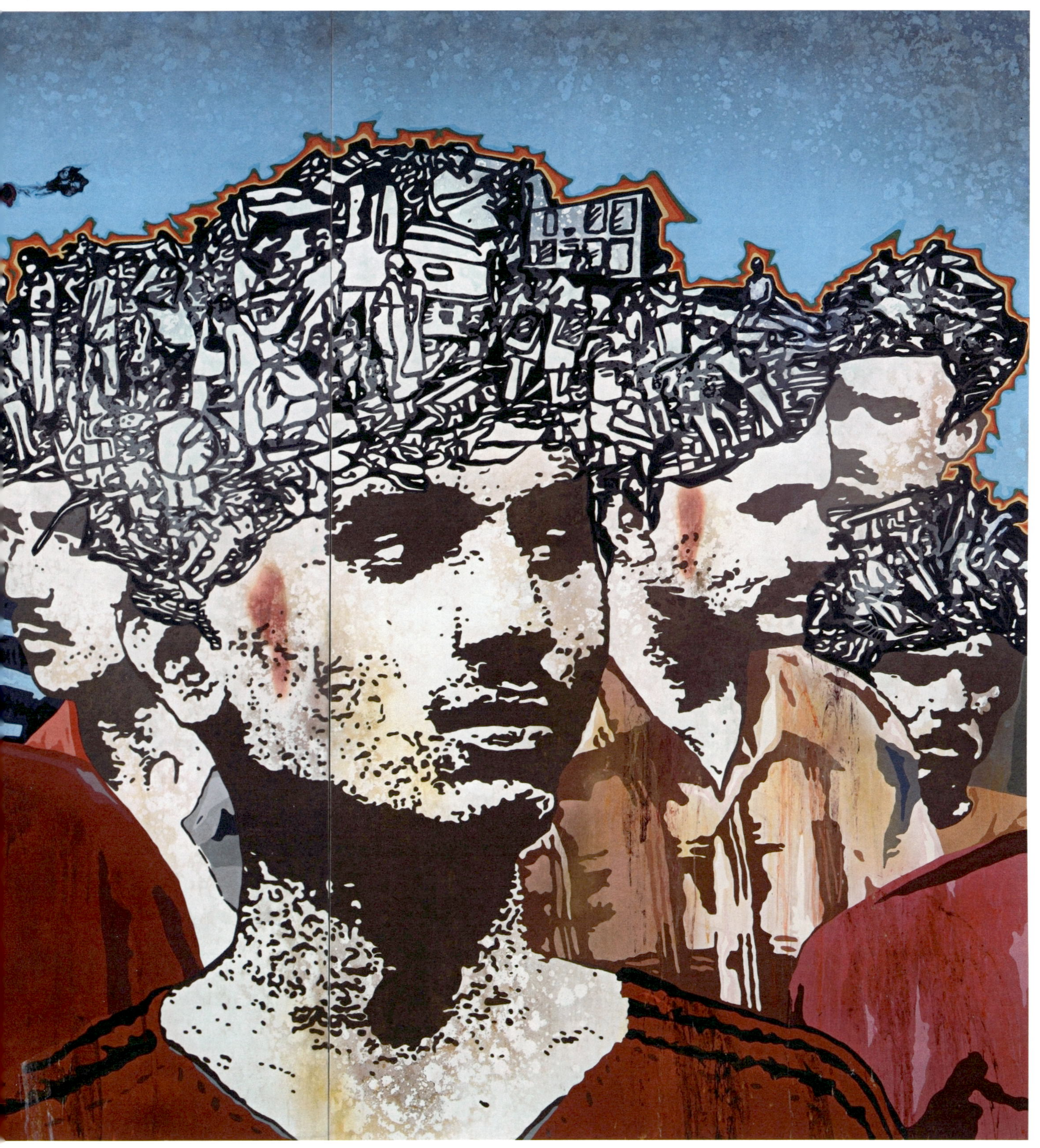

Figure 6
Jitish Kallat,
Sweatopia-1, 2008.
Acrylic on canvas;
274.3 x 518.2 cm
(108 x 204 in.).
Private collection.

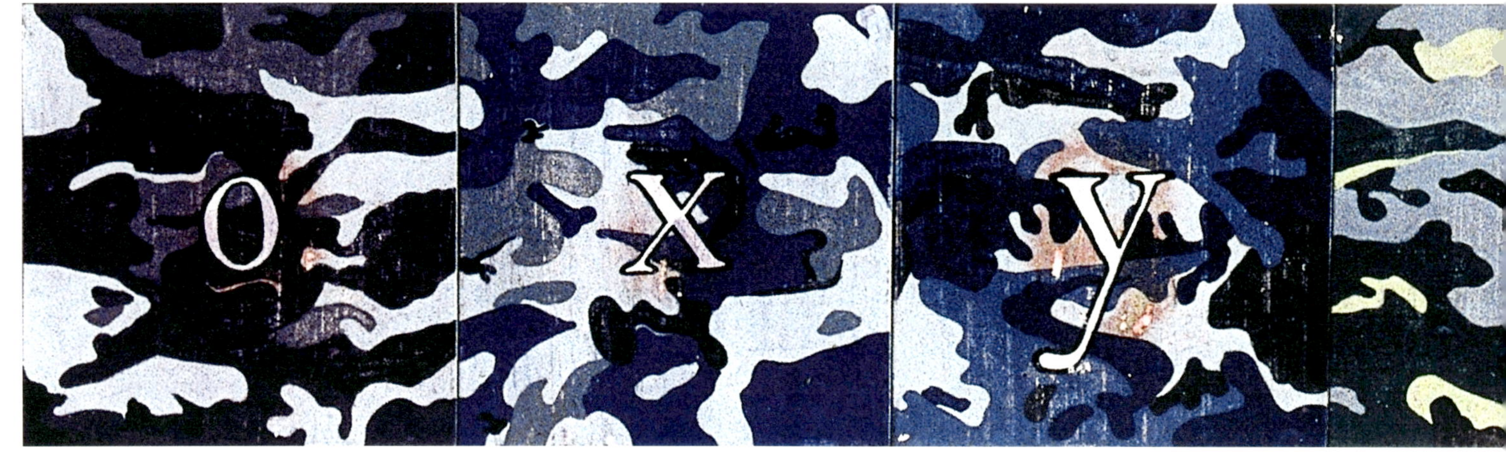

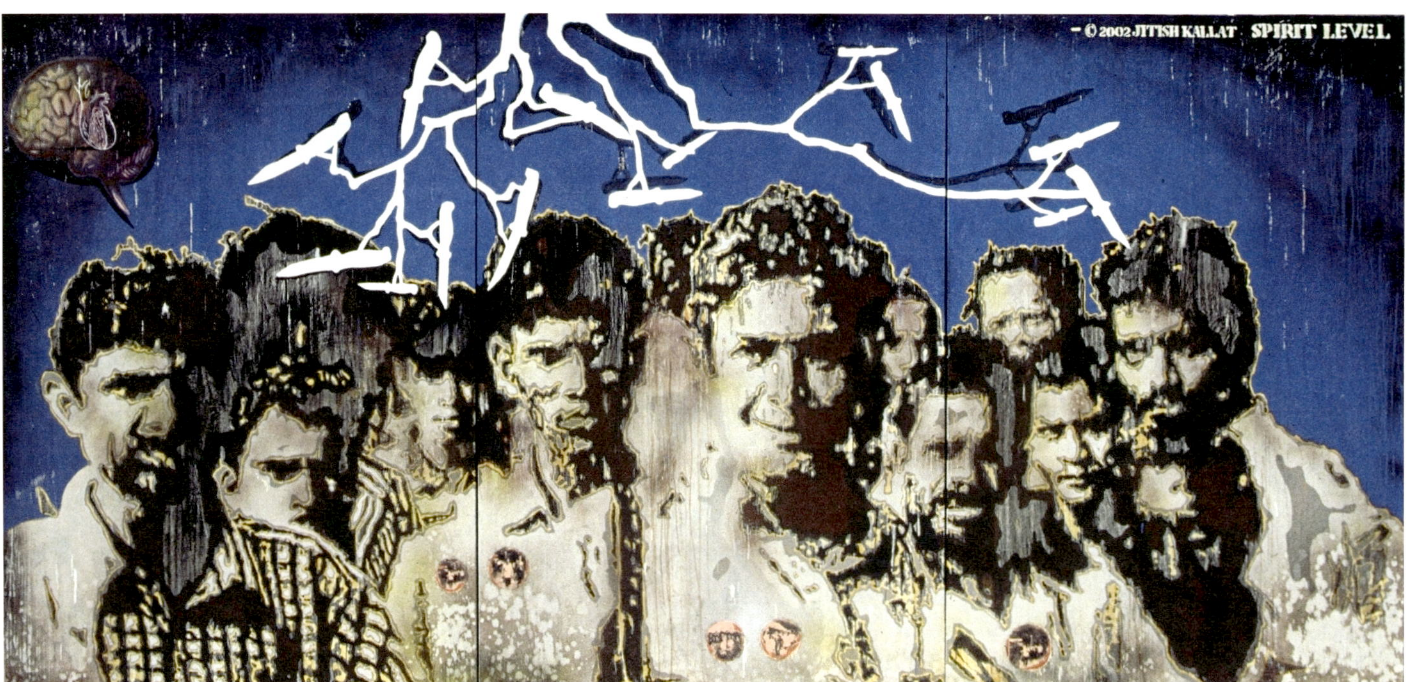

nation of traps, these communicate a boundedness not a gravity, a vox humana of "the individual rendered along with the social web of relationships, memories, experiences . . . [such that] when two or more people come together these images infiltrate each other's space like one conjoined reality."[6]

Figure 8
Jitish Kallat, *Spirit Level*, 2002. Mixed media on canvas; triptych, each panel 228.6 x 457.2 cm (90 x 180 in.). Collection of Amrita Jhaveri, Mumbai.

WHOSE CONJOINED REALITY?

In proposing a set of active and recurring codes, Kallat starts to put forth a need to "hear and see," as in *Tragedienne (Taste, Lick, Swallow and Speak)* (2002; fig. 5), which suggests a communal site or a community that he embellishes with textual references and imploding images that, on an initial, cursory glance, slide and sit evenly, while only at a second look does the whole become uneven and surrealistically improbable. Kallat gathers furtively, mining his imagination in recruiting dimension and ideas. In designing spaces, claiming or speaking for others'

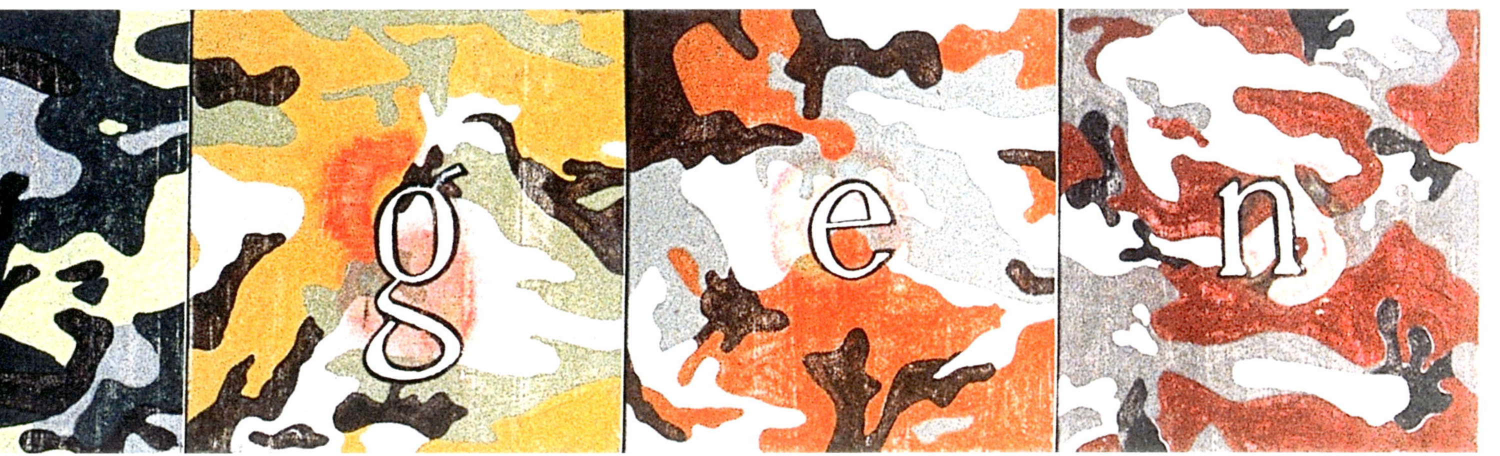

voices, Kallat uses visual influences and codes that suggest things that have consistently fallen between stools and have become the stool pigeons. Women with open mouths, subjects with large spectacles, a suggested near-sightedness, unkept hair, unbuttoned shirts and unchecked saris—slowly but surely, codes in the portraits, as well as in the backgrounds, start to form a specific, terse city on the verge of a subterranean revolution.

Figure 7
Jitish Kallat, *Oxygen*, 2002. Mixed media on canvas; seven panels, each 35.6 x 35.6 cm (14 x 14 in.). Private collection.

THE FIRST DECADE OF THE NEW MILLENNIUM

The murderous violence that has long been received with societal silence and latent care has lately gained sufficient momentum to expose our amnesia culturally and the commonality of our distance from the daily sacrifice of those who fall victim to violence. The measure of this distance is surely found in *Sweatopia-1* (2008; fig. 6): the glazed looks of faces that stare in every direction but at us, showing a stiff bottom lip, gazing nowhere and everywhere. Their grainy necks like a landmass of infected throats, these native Mumbaikars parade the city, fuzzy in their heads and in their hair. The blue evening, with dusky sky, forms an uneven backdrop, casting yet another one of Kallat's inner mythologies—a color reference that suggests the anger and fearful rhythm of the city, its anxious levels and tremulous citizens. The blue hue of *Sweatopia-1* is one that recommends we be guarded in our mode of living in the midst of others. The color combination or plain backgrounds that Kallat employs in many of his paintings have always referred to the color-coded, terrorism-threat advisory scale introduced by the Homeland Security Advisory System in the United States in March 2002—coding that was meant to provide a "comprehensive and effective means to disseminate information regarding the risk of terrorist acts to Federal, State, and local authorities and to the American people."[7] The color coding employed is red for "severe risk of terrorist attacks"; orange for "high" risk; yellow for "elevated" or "significant" risk; blue for "guarded" or "general" risk; and green for "low" risk.

Kallat has made works of art, such as *Oxygen* (2002; fig. 7), wherein the camouflage assumes the colors of these varied threat codes. The notion of the sky as a dangerous canopy appears in other early pieces, including *Spirit Level* (2002; fig. 8), which introduces another sad observation. Here some of the men seem to smile.

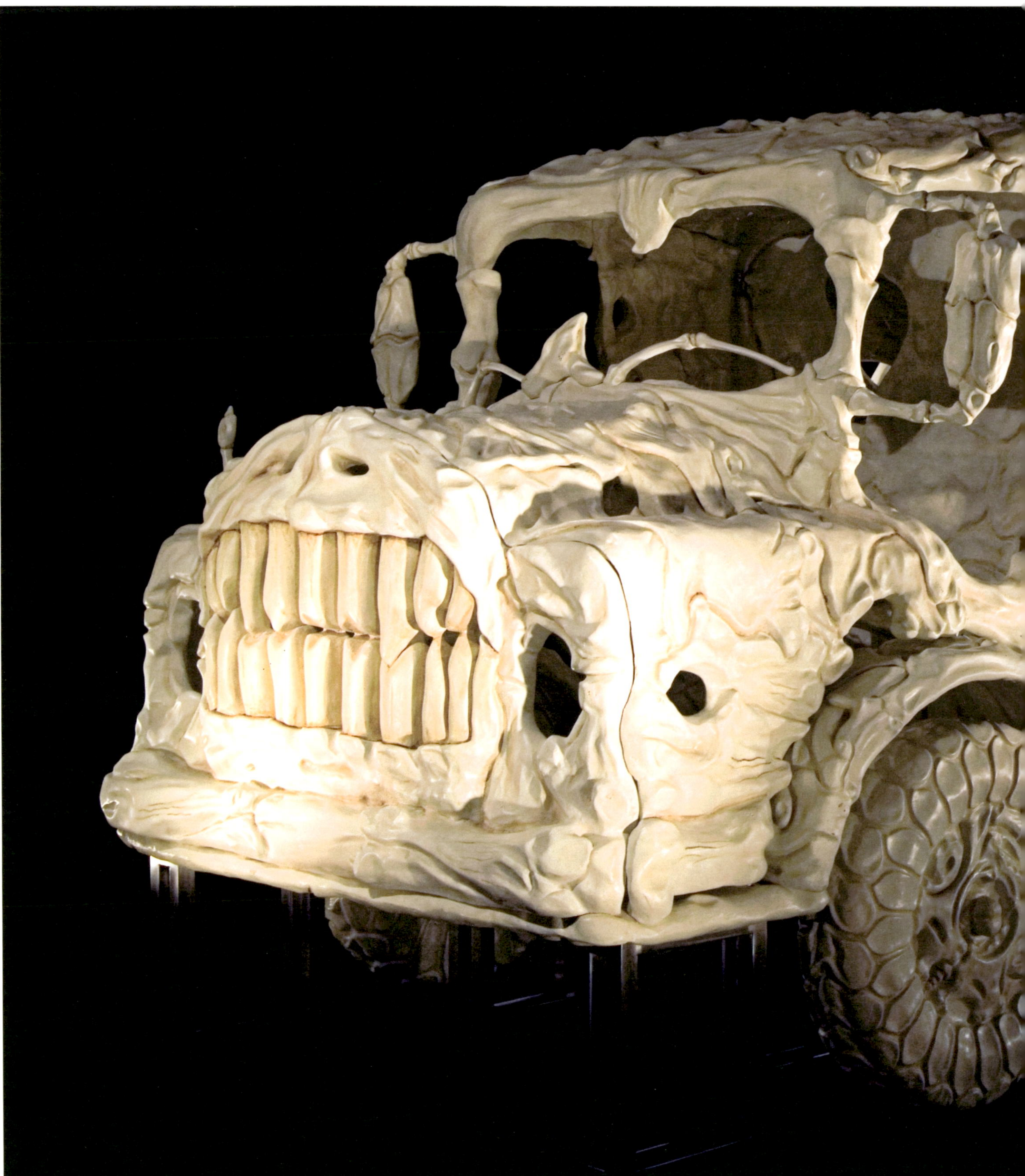

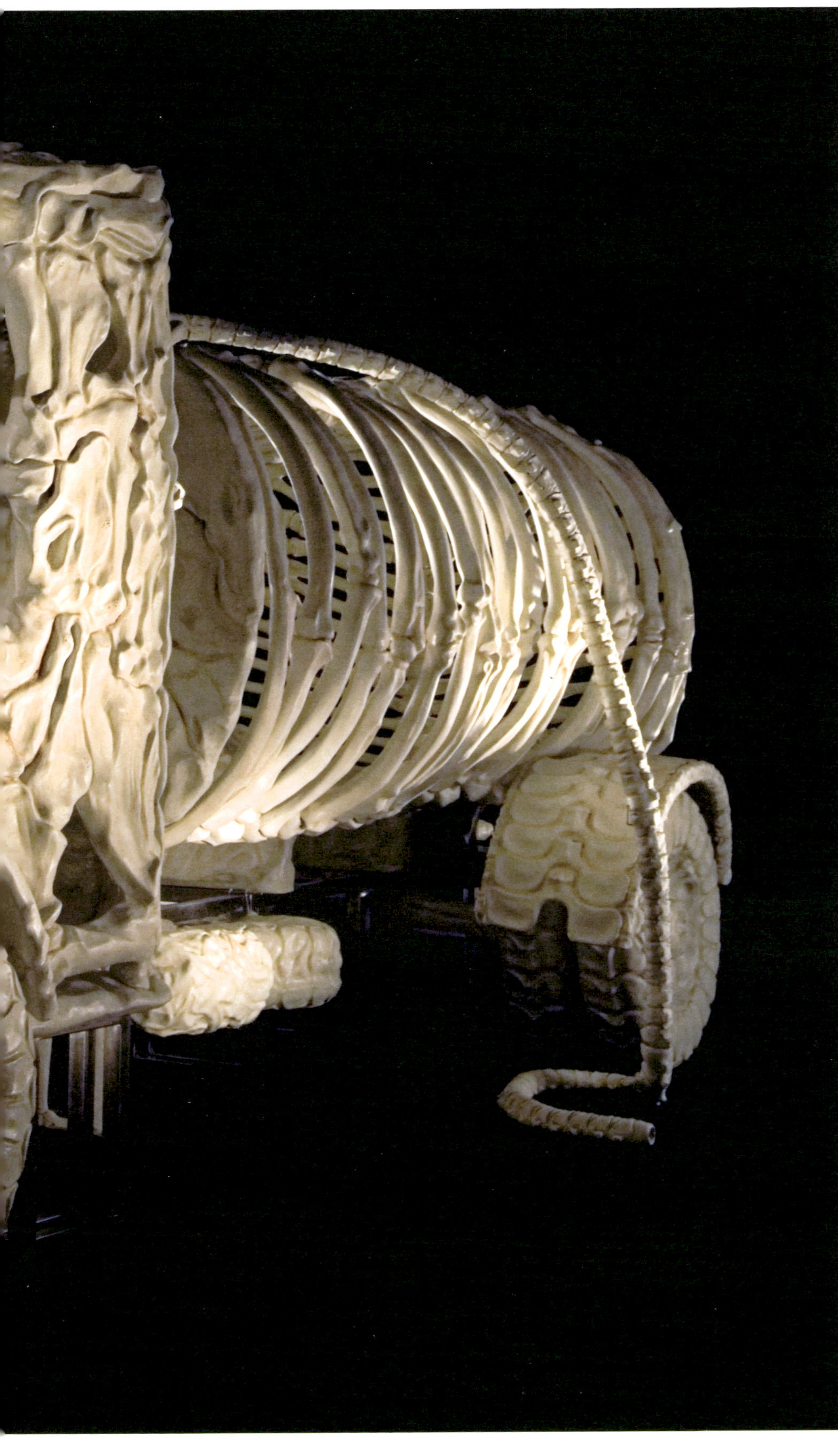

Figure 9
Jitish Kallat,
Aquasaurus, 2008.
Resin, paint, steel;
254 x 688.3 x 269.2
cm (100 x 271 x 106
in.). Private collection.

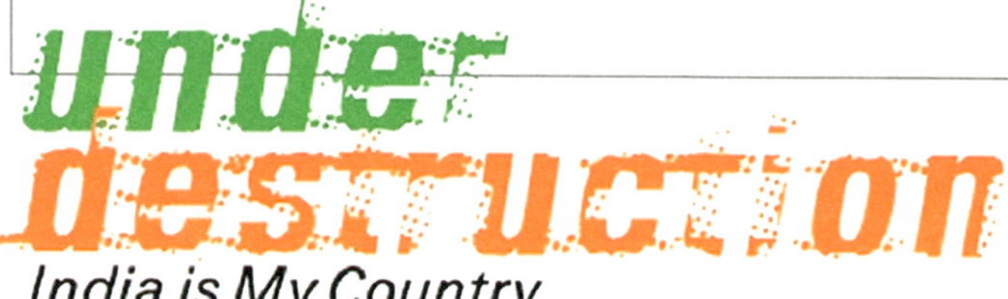

Figure 10
Jitish Kallat, *Under Destruction (India is My Country)*, 2002. Web-based project, part of the *Under Construction: New Dimensions of Asian Art* exhibition at the Japan Foundation Forum Asia Center and the Tokyo Opera City Art Gallery.

Are they happy to be unhappy? Underneath this cracking sky with its volatile lightning strike, have we already come to terms with our indemnity? The flaming horizon line in *Sweatopia-1* (2008) is painted in the four remaining colors of threat level. In a more recent lenticular photowork, *Aspect Ratio* (2009), the seven colors of the rainbow appear and disappear, even if one makes a slight change in one's viewing position, suggesting the momentary possibility of being caught between changing potential risks, high or low, in one step, taken between one breath and another, between two moments, not far apart.

This new rainbow, a coalition of fear, a fundamental of the new order, marks a puritanical observance, on the horizon, that the surety of death follows the plausible violence of active terrorism. An anthropological permanence, formed by an active colorful toolbox, is manufactured in us and about us, through the extraterritoriality of our basic evolutionary and hormone-bound self.

Like a deep-sea diver bringing up remnants forged in fear, Kallat displays an inventiveness from within which we can learn more consciously about the possibilities of our grinding levity. What has become of us, what has become of our countries, we might ask. For Kallat, in his web-based work entitled *Under Destruction (India is My Country)* (2002; fig. 10), the first line, "India is my country," when set in the font known as Wingdings, soon turns into

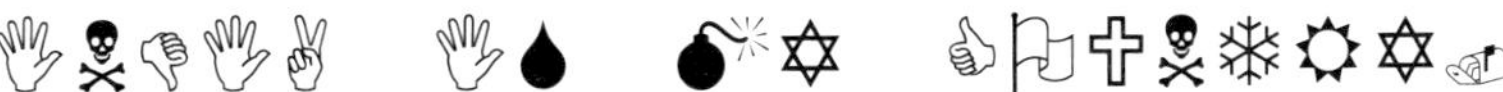

Using Wingdings,[8] which Kallat applied to the foundational pledge of his text, he attempts to apply the very conditions of unanswered and unexplained, if yet quickly merging, realities and myths to real events in the world, especially those surrounding and preceding the 9/11/2001 attacks in New York and Washington that appeared on the internet.[9] The often prolific, emotively rife and viral language of gossip and mythmaking, using symbolic and recognizable gestures, provides another leveling tool to understand a global situation that affects the national notion of belonging and safety. The work is an ode to the power of creative query within the unknown and the unanswered, which remains our daily bedfellow in a world now dominated by hurt and the unfurling of flags and logos, and little real debate.

The air smells...of fear, anxiety, and simplicity.
Marieta Maglas[10]

THE HISTORICAL TEXT AND THE VITUPERATION OF EVERYTHING/OTHER

Historical texts are important milestones that feed into many aspects of our national and political horizons, but recently, much diverse material has been used to create the usual moral panics and dichotomies, including the perversion of historical material that can include these milestone texts. From charters of freedom to declarations of independence, from the constitution of empires to the narratives of life (on slavery) and to models of Christian charity, historical texts of all sorts—and even prose and poems that are cited as historical texts—have been used to proscribe and yet they make, arguably, a broader Eurocentric argument for the defense of liberal politics within the notion of enlightenment. A *modus vivendi* of stainless modernity

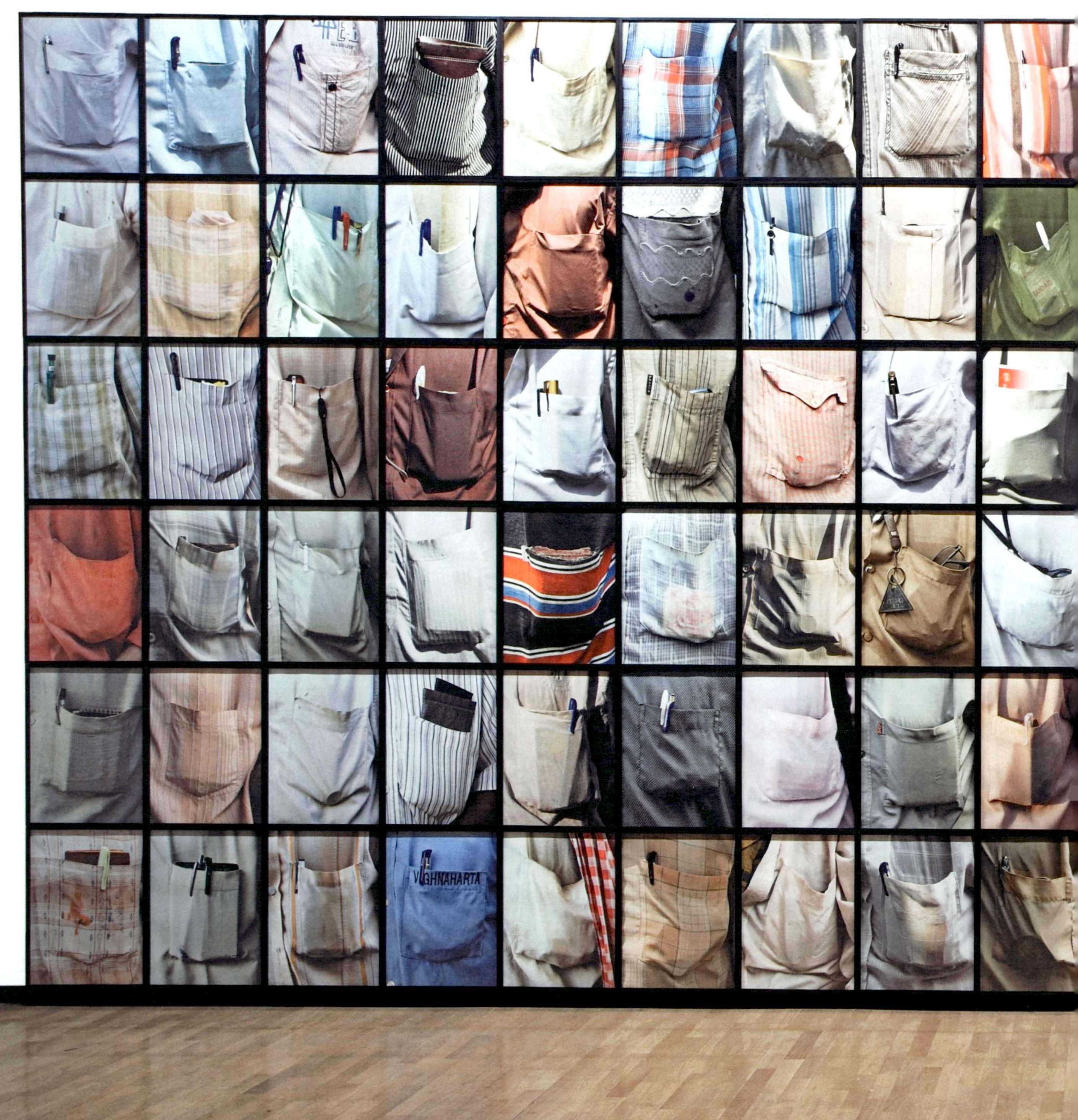

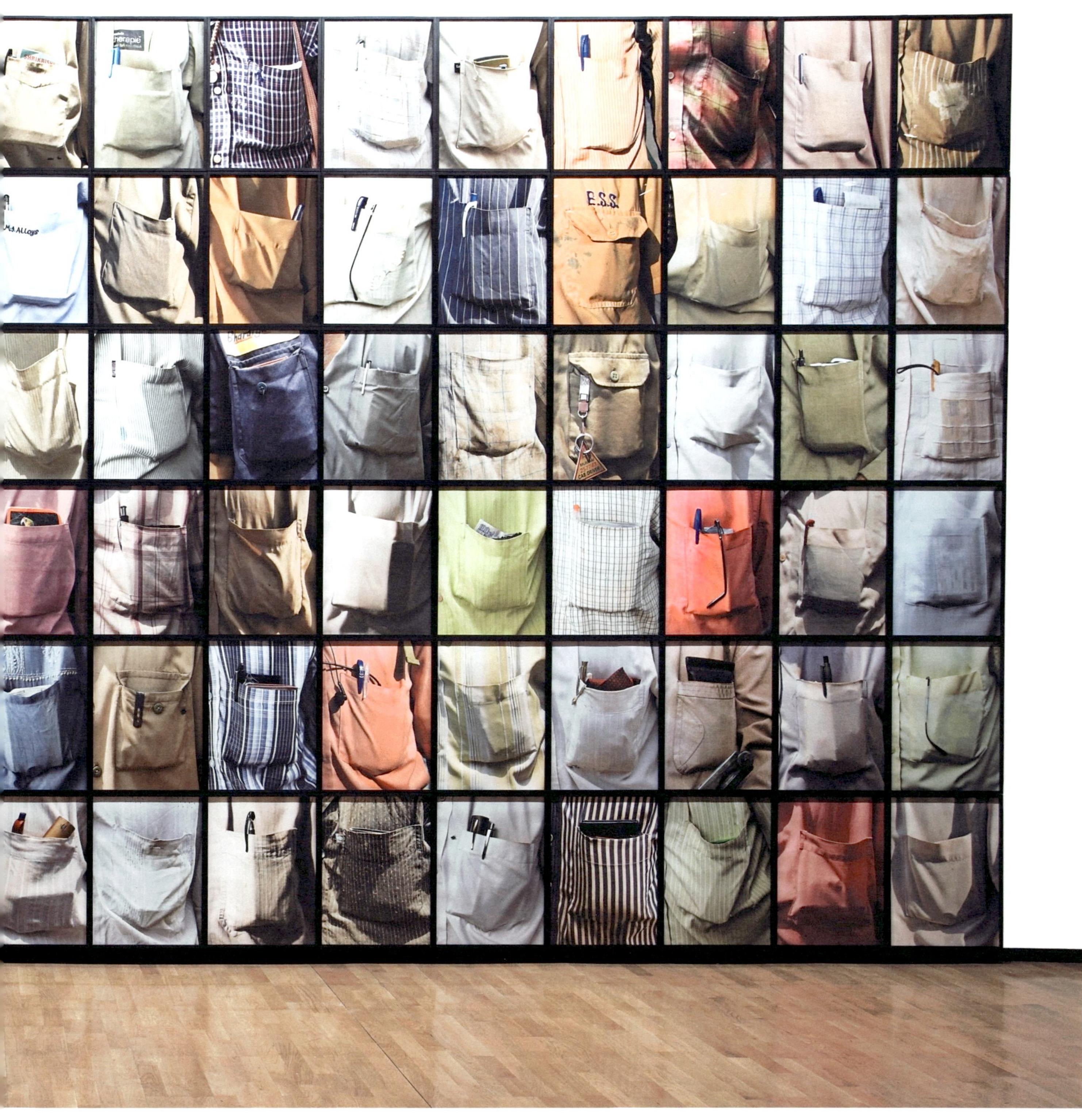

is still empowered against a background of a growing fanaticism, creeping about in the guise of a political religiosity, understood as irrational absolutism. The current conjunction and diachronic implications of these historical texts, as they are cited to evoke the battle between extremism and secular values, further fill a bedazzled globe with accusatory probabilities and fears of the loss of emancipating possibilities. The ongoing implications of democratic engagements and projects have invaluably, and vehemently, been debated by luminaries of philosophy, including Slavoj Zizek and Alberto Toscano, often giving light and inspiration to others.

As such, Kallat asks in his *Public Notice* (2003) project, "What are the terms of the debate?"[11] He makes text into image at a time when political debate has become regressive and our understanding of secularism has been to the exclusion of those deemed "fundamental" or even fanatically religious. In this environment, historical texts recur and are uploaded as part of the process of othering that makes the bias of communities a serious viral veneer of democratic appeal and security.

In the experience of reading, moving, and feeling the pulse and passion of words, Kallat casts another net—one that helps us to understand these texts in their time and in their potential. Liberties are expounded and alphabets are shown as notations, while events are portrayed as contemporary. The treatment of the individual letters—whether burned onto mirrors as in *Public Notice* or cast in bones for *Public Notice 2* or even rendered in the color-coded, terrorism-threat advisory scale for *Public Notice 3*—are typographical variations by which to create an extreme graphic impact on the reader's attention. All three works exhibit a concrete poetry in which the physical arrangements of words are used to help suggest the artist's meaning as a theme. A baroque installation with frugal means makes visible the humane and liberal limits of that which we have lost, are (in)visibly losing, and that which we are slaying. In an era of subdued genocides, highly spirited ideologies, and unilateral rationalizing "after the execution," we are left but to ponder on these texts, for what we can glean from them, from how they can influence us now. Most importantly, these three texts all speak of recent memory as historic moments that can help us to retain and address resistance. Kallat makes these texts as physical borders that help us to negotiate the function of history and memory in our world that obliterates so much, so quickly, through a repetition of trauma and by meditating on the infinite possibilities of an ecology of fear.

As Tocqueville said of the French revolutionary ideology, it is a "armed opinion."[12] As Kallat states in his work *Conditions Apply* (2005), even the moon has become rationed and used for fodder. And as Muhamad Iqbal has written, "Become dust—and they will throw thee in the air; become stone—and they will throw thee on glass."[13]

Shaheen Merali is an independent curator and art critic living in London.

NOTES

1. Mina Loy, "Gertrude Stein," in *Transatlantic Review* 2.3 (Yale University, Beinecke Library, Mina Loy Papers, October 1924), pp. 429–30.

2. Kabir, "Abode of the Beloved," in *Poems by Kabir,* http://www.poemhunter.com/poem/abode-of-the-beloved/.

3. Shaheen Merali in conversation with Jitish Kallat, in *Jitish Kallat, Public Notice 2*, edited by Shaheen Merali, exh. cat. (Bodhi Art, Singapore, 2008), p. 16.

4. Laura Kipnis, "Repossessing Popular Culture," in *Theory in Contemporary Art Since 1985*, edited by Zoya Kocur and Simon Leung (Blackwell Publishing, 2005), p. 373.

5. This and the proceeding paragraph appeared in substantially the same form in Shaheen Merali, "Guilt Gilded in Gold," in *India Contemporary: Jitish Kallat, Sudarshan Shetty, Riyas Komu*, edited by Laura Stamps and Janey Tucker, exh. cat. (GEM Museum of Contemporary Art, 2009), pp. 21–22.

6. Shaheen Merali, e-mail conversation with Jitish Kallat, July 31, 2010.

7. See http://en.wikipedia.org/wiki/Homeland_Security_Advisory_System#History.

8. Wingdings is a TrueType dingbat font included in all versions of Microsoft Windows starting with version 3.1. The Wingdings trademark is owned by Microsoft, and the glyph order was patented. This font contains many widely familiar shapes and gestures, as well as some recognized world symbols such as the Star of David and the symbols of the Zodiac. The font is not mapped to Unicode, although many of its symbols are available in that system; see http://en.wikipedia.org/wiki/Wingdings.

9. The complete text reads as follows:

> INDIA IS MY COUNTRY.
> ALL INDIANS ARE MY BROTHERS AND SISTERS.
> I LOVE MY COUNTRY AND I'M PROUD OF ITS RICH AND VARIED HERITAGE.
> I SHALL ALWAYS TRY TO BE WORTHY OF IT.
> I SHALL GIVE MY PARENTS, TEACHERS AND ALL ELDERS RESPECT AND TREAT EVERYONE
> WITH COURTESY.
> TO MY COUNTRY AND ITS PEOPLE, I PLEDGE MY DEVOTION.
> IN THEIR WELL BEING AND PROSPERITY ALONE LIES MY HAPPINESS.

10. Marieta Maglas, "In the same space (Concrete poetry)," in *Poems by Marieta Maglas,* http://www.poemhunter.com/poem/in-the-same-space-concrete-poetry/.

11. Shaheen Merali, e-mail conversation with Jitish Kallat, July 31, 2010.

12. Richard Seymour, "Alberto Toscano on Fanaticism," in *Lenin's Tomb*, http://leninology.blogspot.com/2010/07/alberto-toscano-on-fanaticism.html.

13. Muhamad Iqbal, see http://www.brainyquote.com/quotes/quotes/m/muhammadiq204891.html.

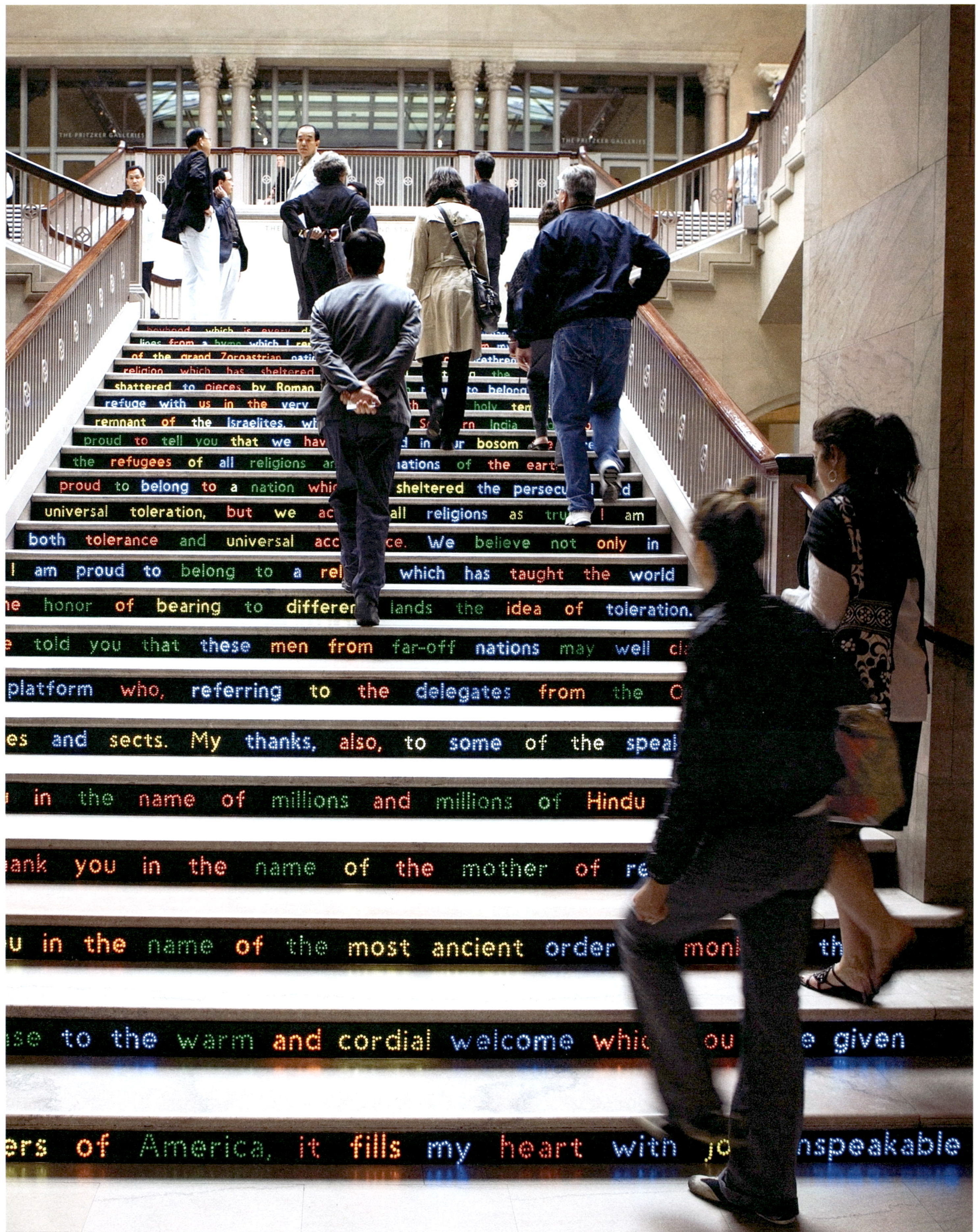

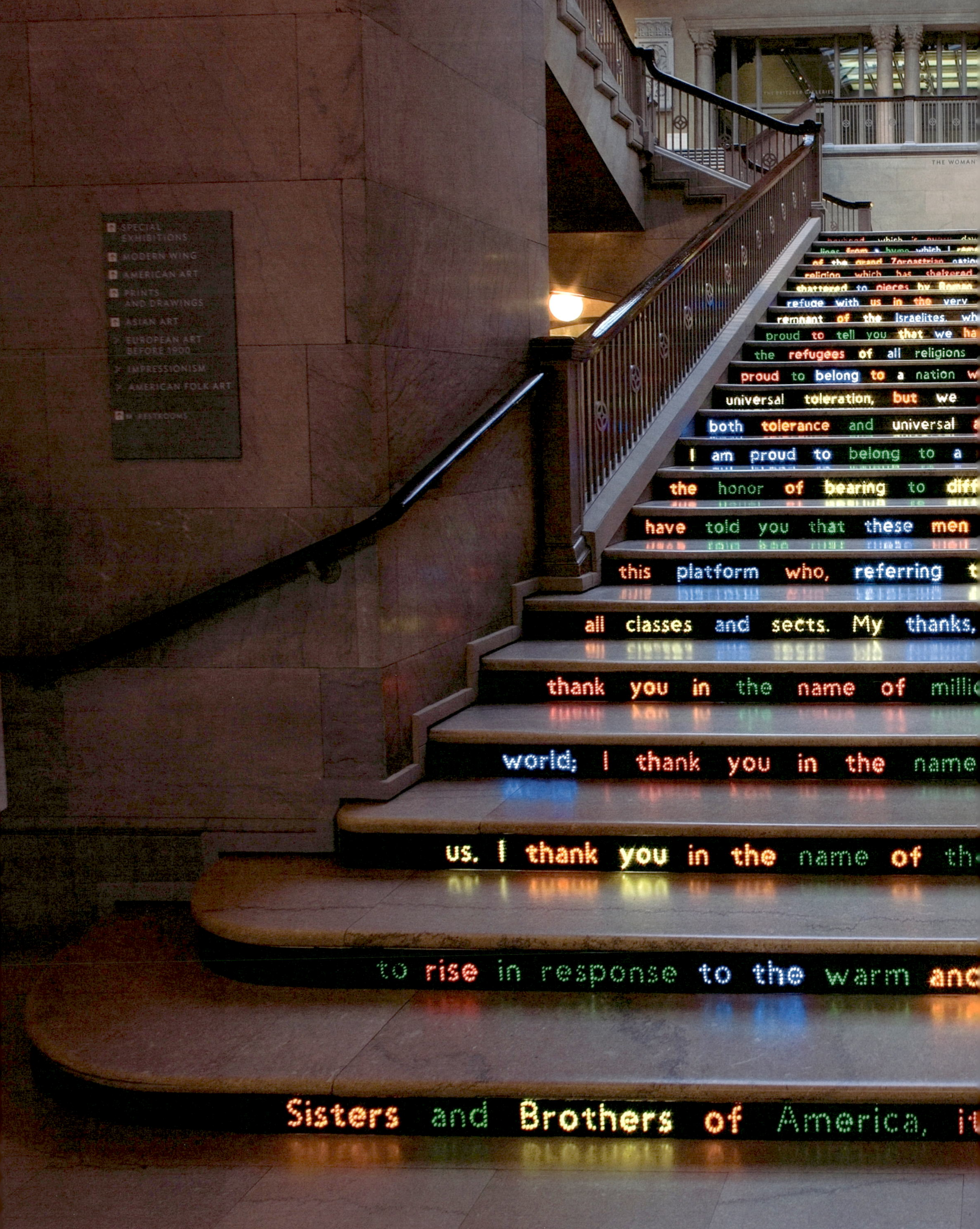
SPECIAL
EXHIBITIONS
MODERN WING
AMERICAN ART
PRINTS
AND DRAWINGS
ASIAN ART
EUROPEAN ART
BEFORE 1900
IMPRESSIONISM
AMERICAN FOLK ART
RESTROOMS
lines from a hymn which I rem
of the grand Zoroastrian natio
religion which has sheltered
shattered to pieces by Roman
refuge with us in the very
remnant of the Israelites, wh
proud to tell you that we ha
the refugees of all religions
proud to belong to a nation w
universal toleration, but we
both tolerance and universal a
I am proud to belong to a
the honor of bearing to diff
have told you that these men
this platform who, referring t
all classes and sects. My thanks,
thank you in the name of milli
world; I thank you in the name
us. I thank you in the name of th
to rise in response to the warm and
Sisters and Brothers of America, it

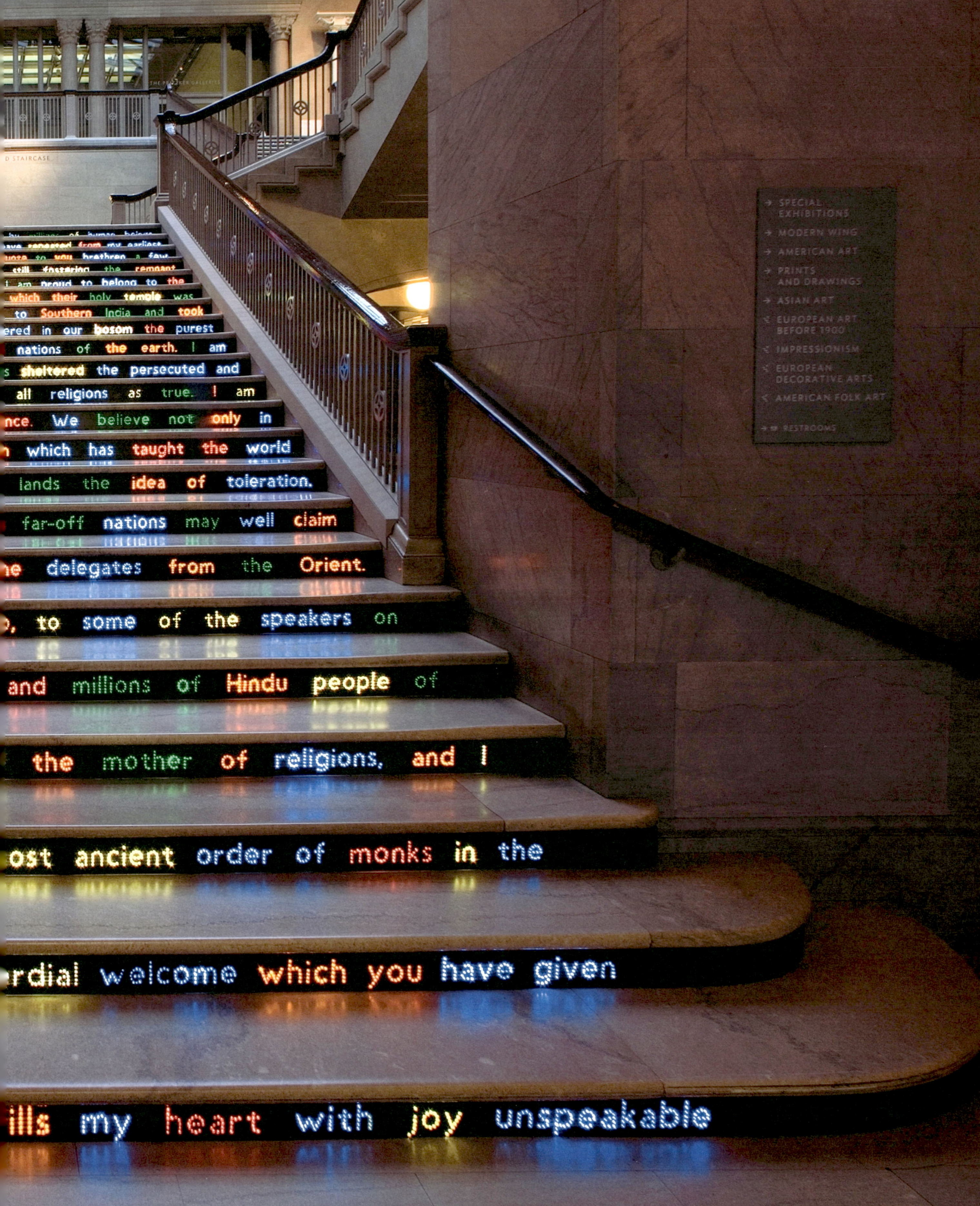
by millions of human beings
have separated from my earliest
unto you brethren a few
still fostering the remnant
I am proud to belong to the
which their holy temple was
to Southern India and took
ered in our bosom the purest
nations of the earth. I am
sheltered the persecuted and
all religions as true. I am
nce. We believe not only in
which has taught the world
lands the idea of toleration.
far-off nations may well claim
delegates from the Orient.
to some of the speakers on
and millions of Hindu people of
the mother of religions, and I
ost ancient order of monks in the
rdial welcome which you have given
ills my heart with joy unspeakable

SPECIAL
EXHIBITIONS
MODERN WING
AMERICAN ART
PRINTS
AND DRAWINGS
ASIAN ART
EUROPEAN ART
BEFORE 1900
IMPRESSIONISM
EUROPEAN
DECORATIVE ARTS
AMERICAN FOLK ART
RESTROOMS

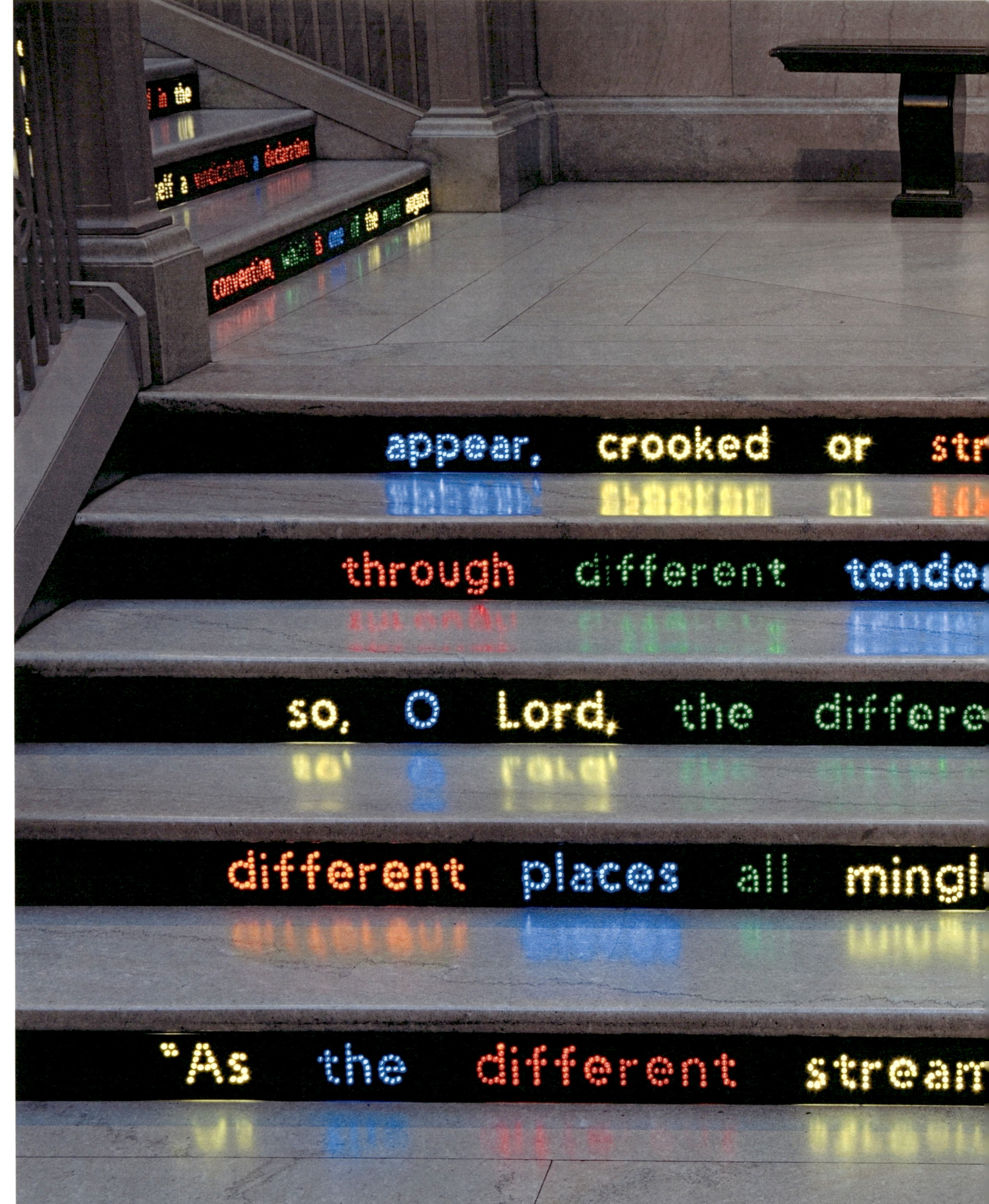

appear, crooked or str
through different tende
so, O Lord, the differe
different places all mingl
"As the different stream

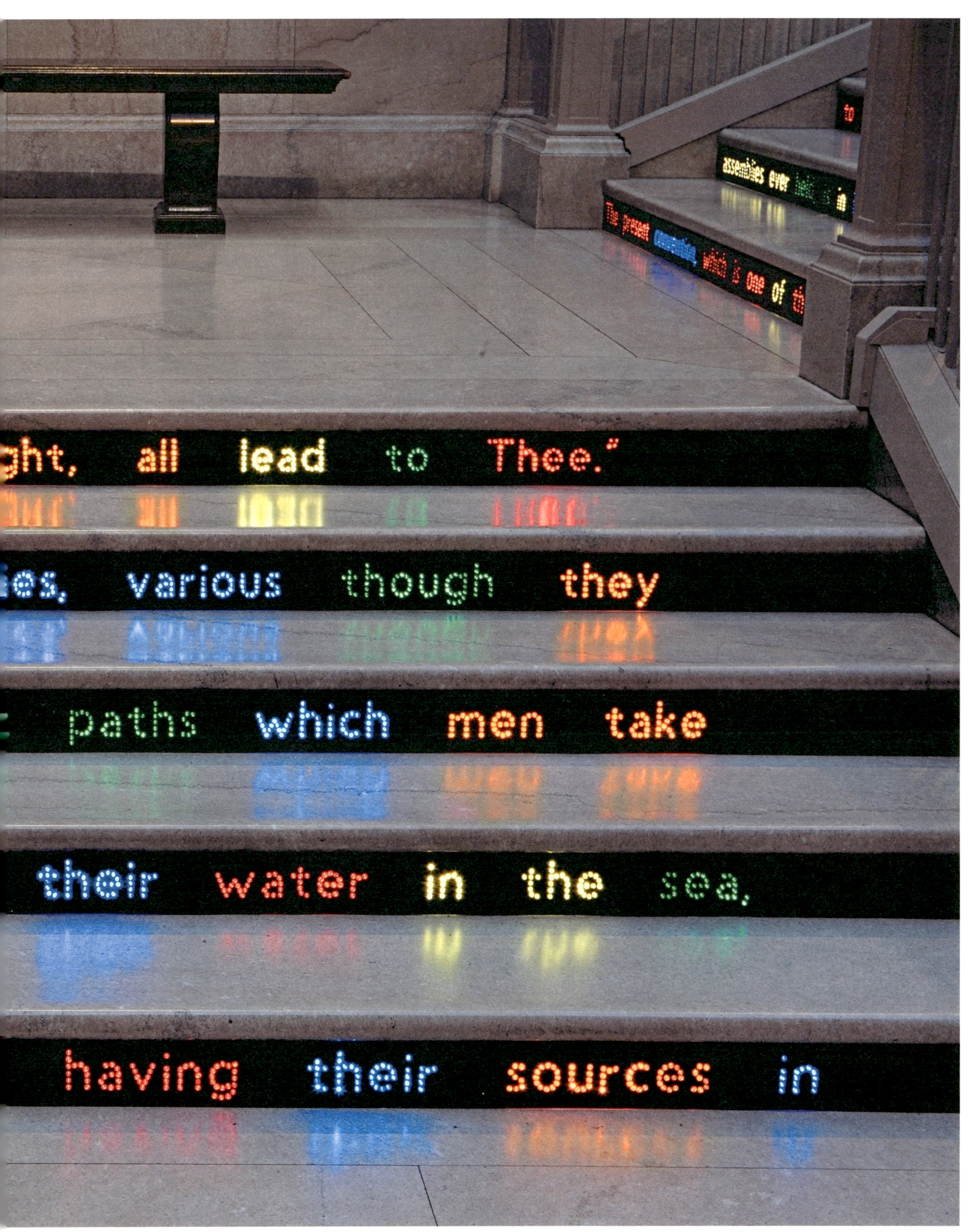
assemblies over
to
The present assemblies which is one of th
ght, all lead to Thee."
es, various though they
paths which men take
their water in the sea,
having their sources in

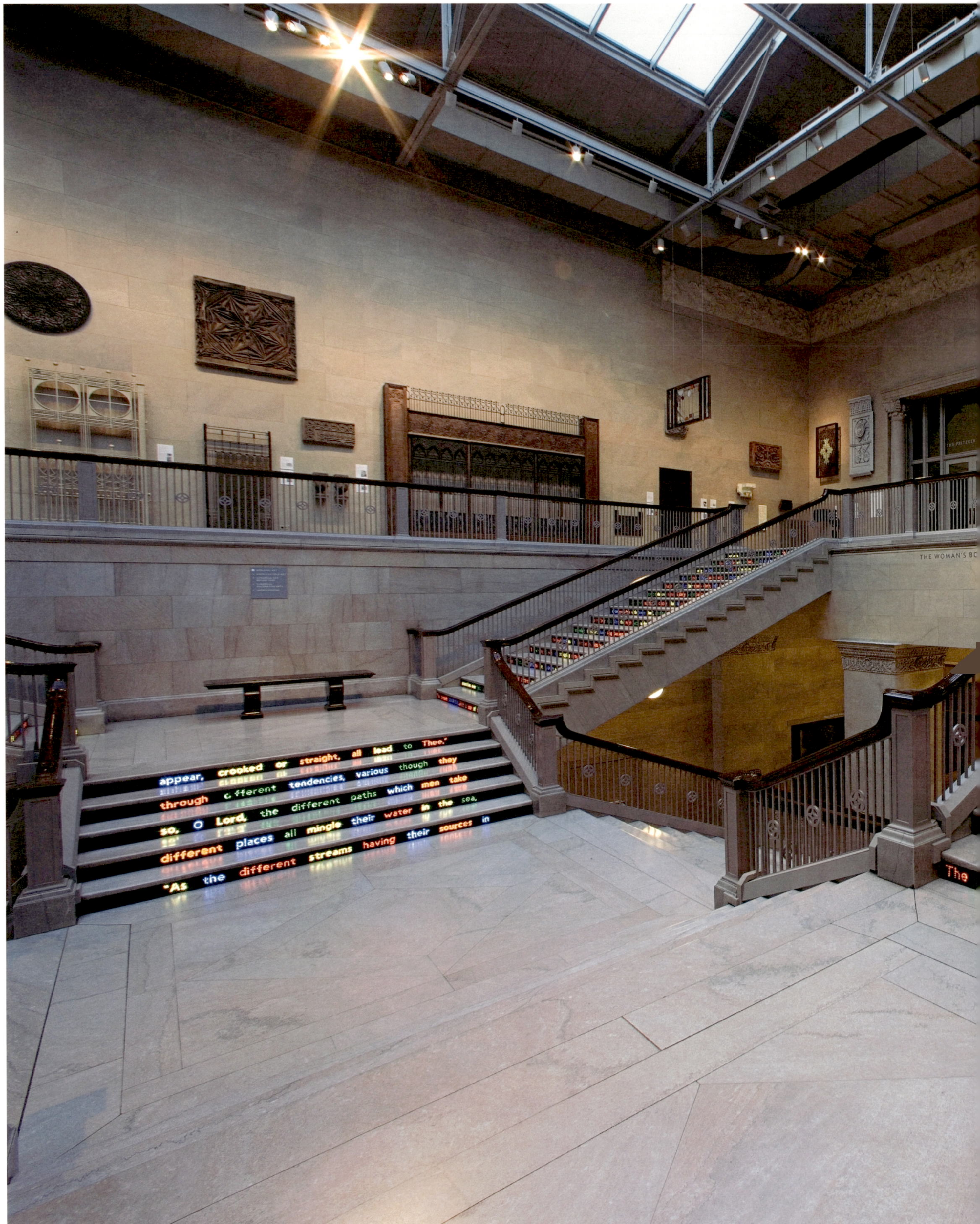
appear, crooked or straight, all lead to Thee."
through different tendencies, various though they
so, O Lord, the different paths which men take
different places all mingle their water in the sea,
"As the different streams having their sources in
THE WOMAN'S BO
THE PRITZKE

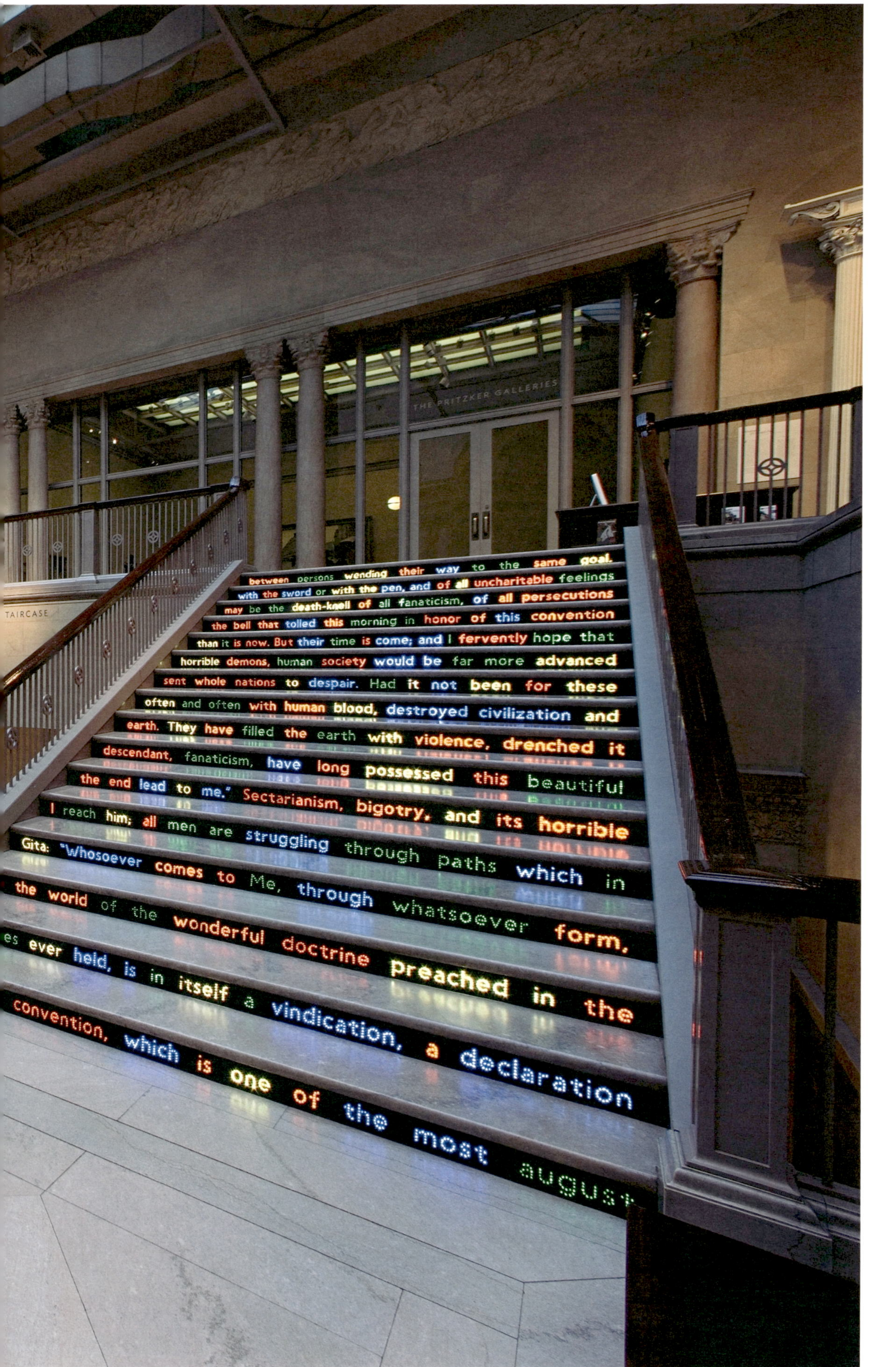
THE PRITZKER GALLERIES
TAIRCASE
between persons wending their way to the same goal,
with the sword or with the pen, and of all uncharitable feelings
may be the death-knell of all fanaticism, of all persecutions
the bell that tolled this morning in honor of this convention
than it is now. But their time is come; and I fervently hope that
horrible demons, human society would be far more advanced
sent whole nations to despair. Had it not been for these
often and often with human blood, destroyed civilization and
earth. They have filled the earth with violence, drenched it
descendant, fanaticism, have long possessed this beautiful
the end lead to me." Sectarianism, bigotry, and its horrible
I reach him; all men are struggling through paths which in
Gita: "Whosoever comes to Me, through whatsoever form,
the world of the wonderful doctrine preached in the
es ever held, is in itself a vindication, a declaration
convention, which is one of the most
august

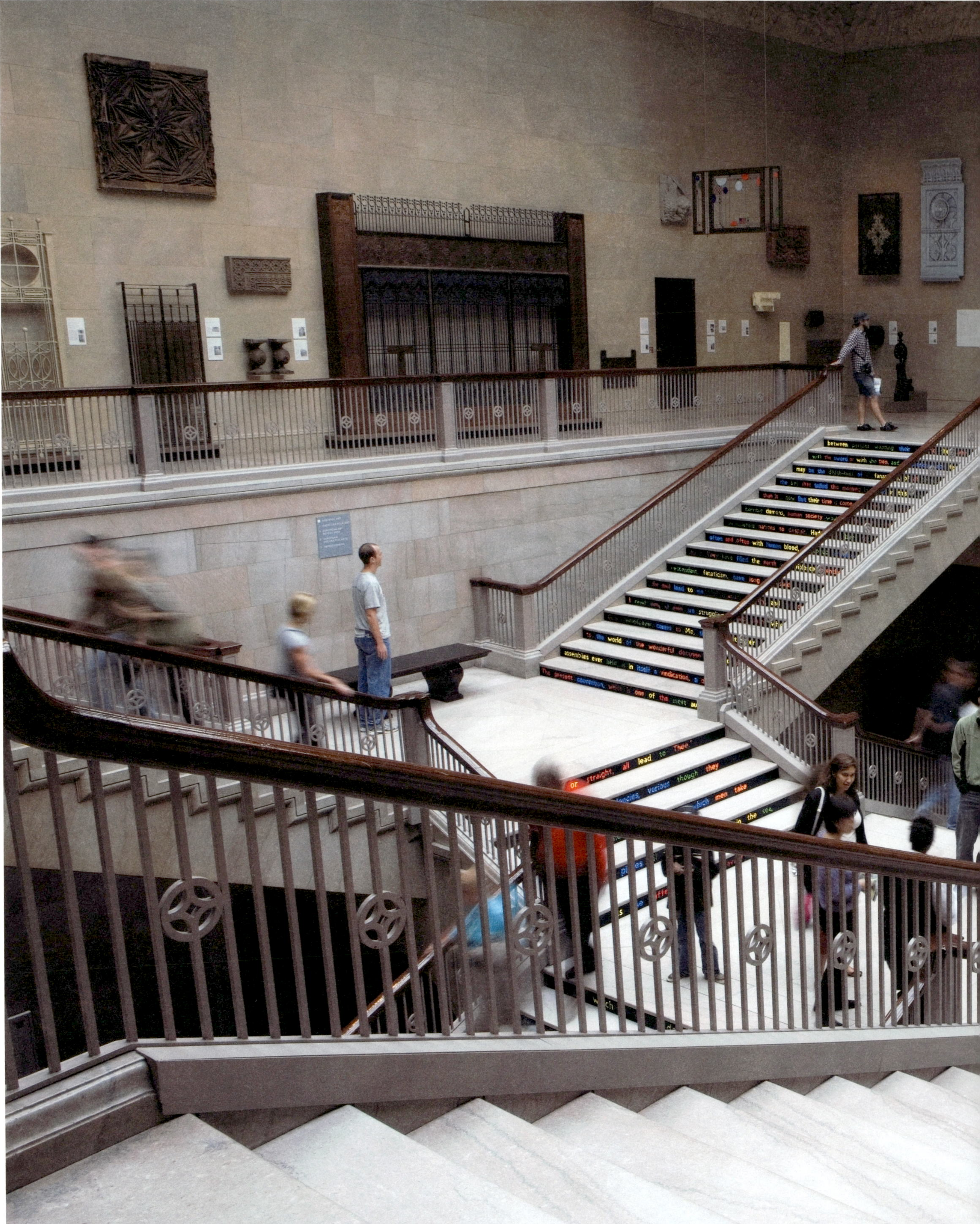

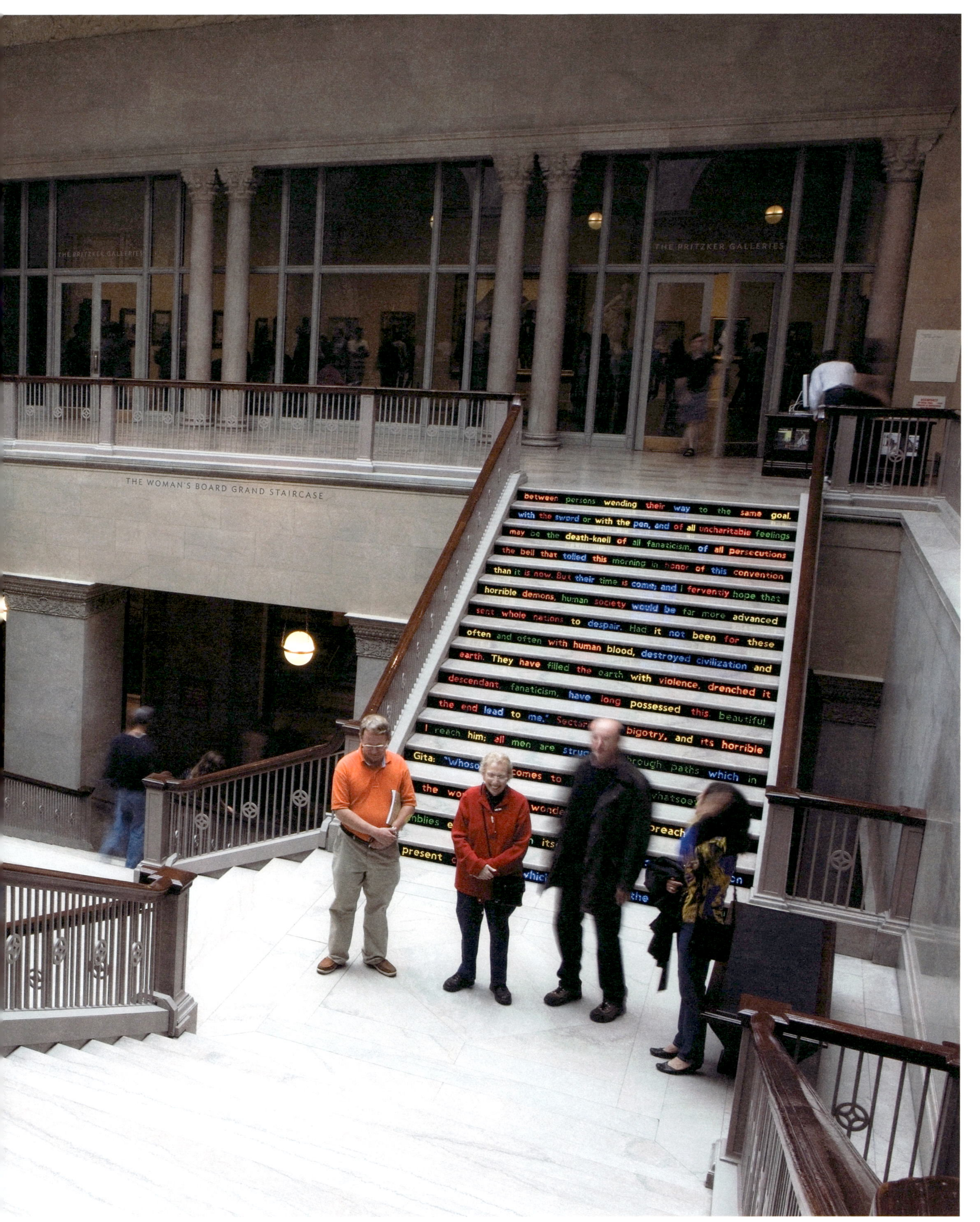

THE PRITZKER GALLERIES
THE PRITZKER GALLERIES
THE WOMAN'S BOARD GRAND STAIRCASE
between persons wending their way to the same goal.
with the sword or with the pen, and of all uncharitable feelings
may be the death-knell of all fanaticism, of all persecutions
the bell that tolled this morning in honor of this convention
than it is now. But their time is come; and I fervently hope that
horrible demons, human society would be far more advanced
sent whole nations to despair. Had it not been for these
often and often with human blood, destroyed civilization and
earth. They have filled the earth with violence, drenched it
descendant, fanaticism, have long possessed this beautiful!
the end lead to me." Sectarianism, bigotry, and its horrible
I reach him; all men are struggling through paths which in
Gita: "Whosoever comes to me
the world
blies
present
which
the

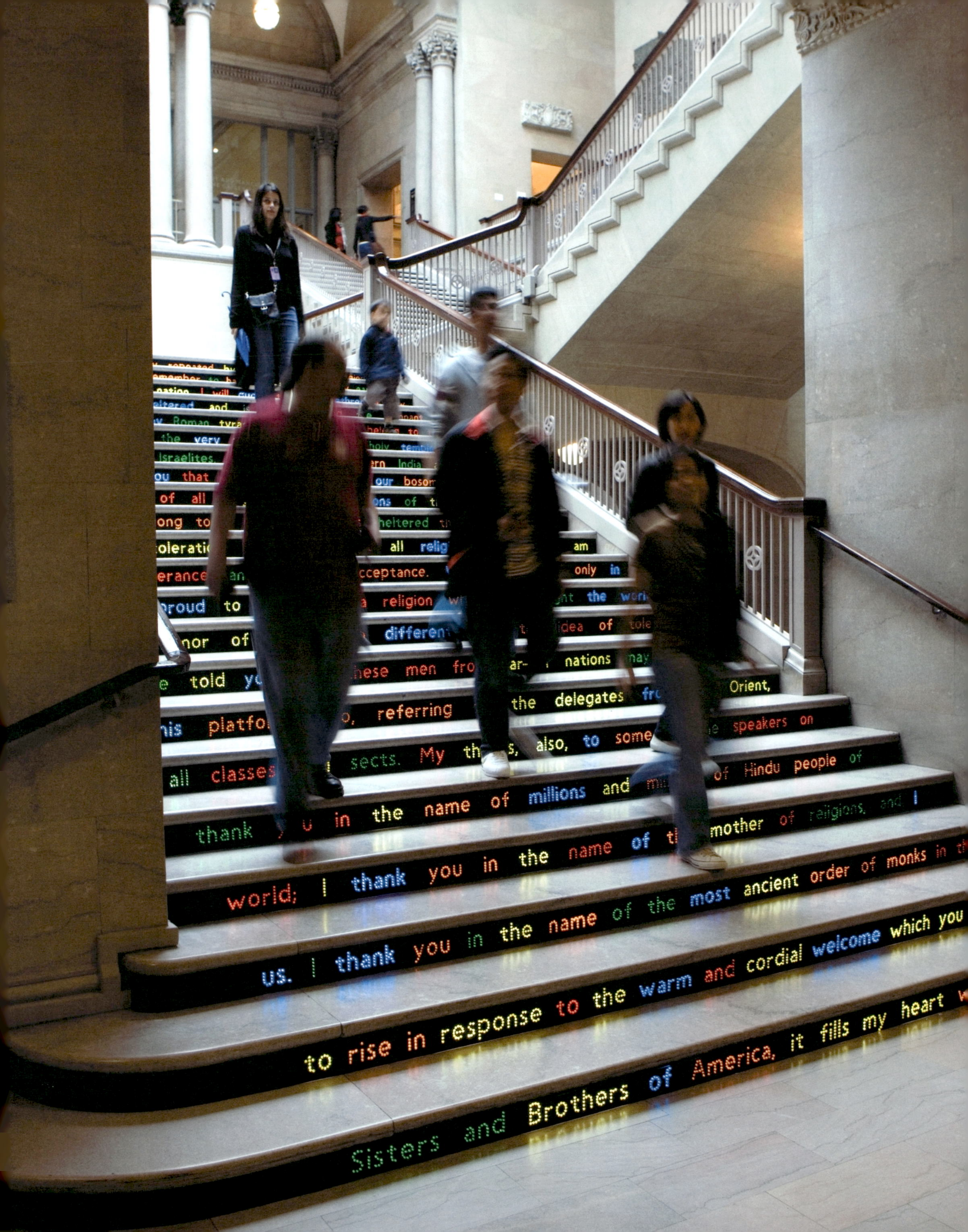
Sisters and Brothers of America, it fills my heart w
to rise in response to the warm and cordial welcome which you
us. I thank you in the name of the most ancient order of monks in th
world; I thank you in the name of the mother of religions, and I
thank you in the name of millions and mi of Hindu people of
all classes sects. My th s, also, to some e speakers on
his platfor o, referring the delegates fr Orient,
told y hese men fro ar nations may
nor of different idea of tole
proud to religion wh ght the worl
erance an cceptance. only in
oleratio all religi am
ong to heltered th
of all ns of t
you that our bosom
Israelites holy temp ern India
the very
y Roman tyra
eltered and is
nation I will
emember to h
repeated b

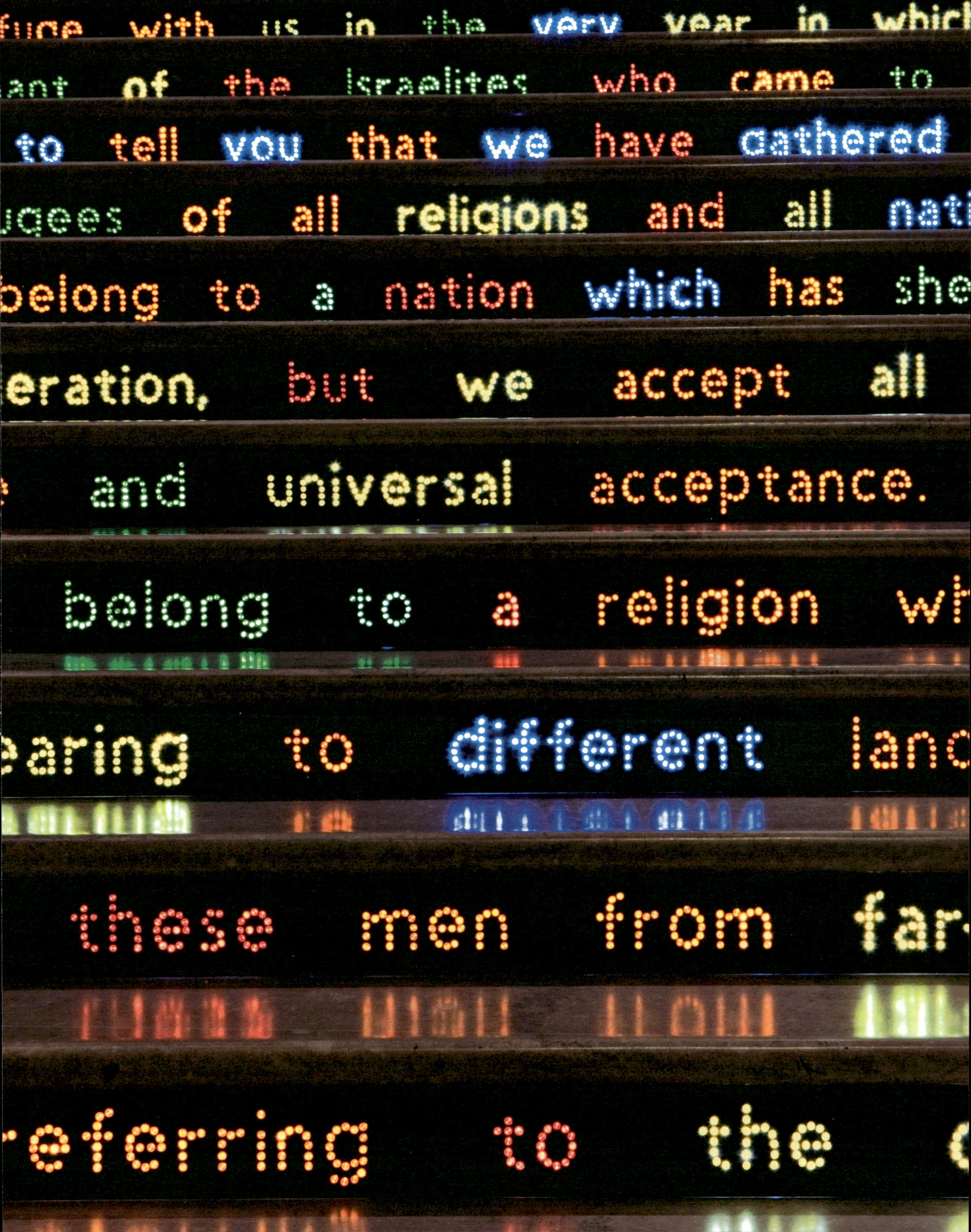

fuge with us in the very year in which
ant of the Israelites who came to
to tell you that we have gathered
ugees of all religions and all nati
belong to a nation which has she
eration, but we accept all
and universal acceptance.
belong to a religion wh
earing to different lan
these men from far
referring to the

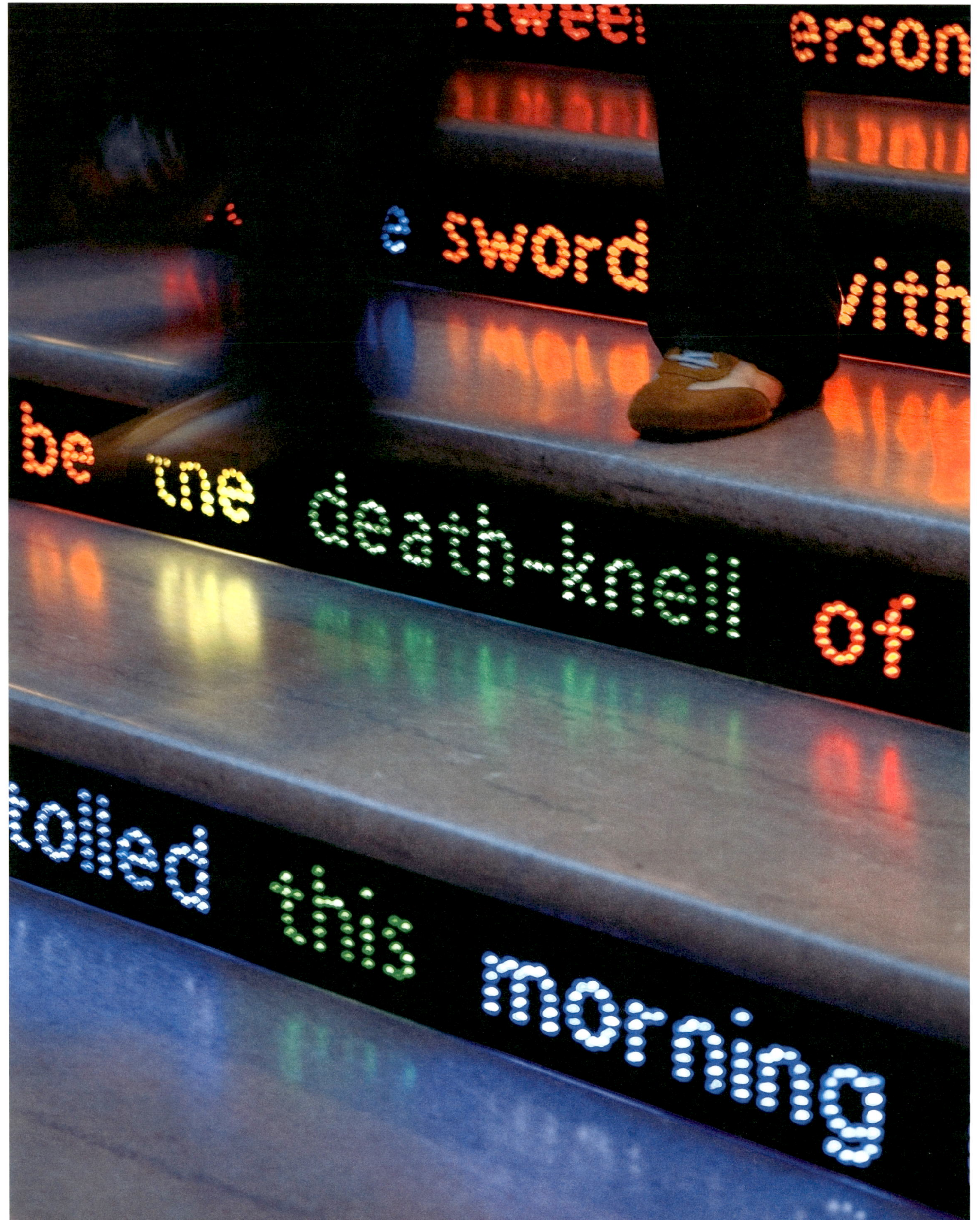
twee
erson
e sword
vith
be the death-knell of
oiled this morning

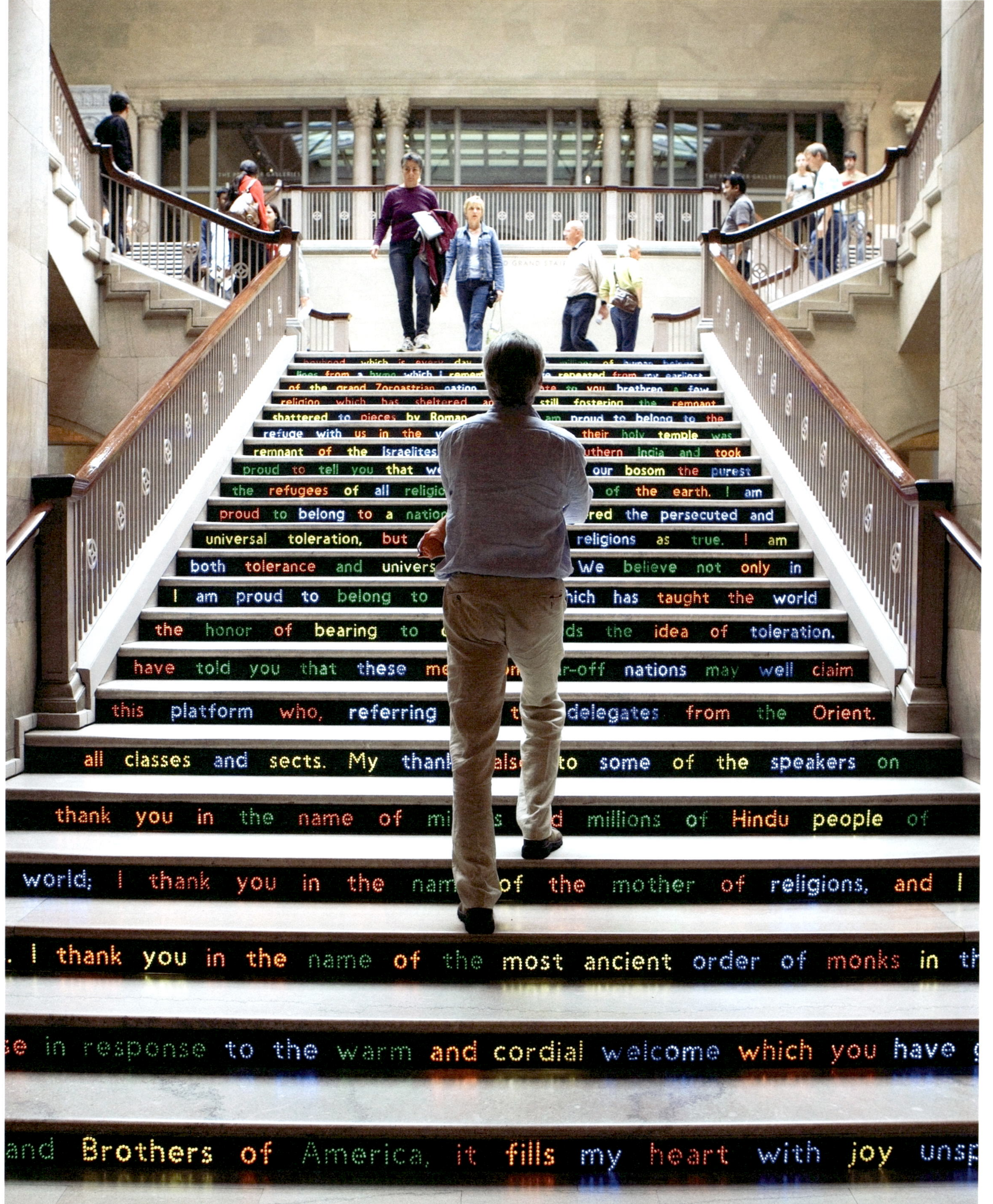
boyhood which is every day millions of human beings
lines from a hymn which I remember repeated from my earliest
of the grand Zoroastrian nation date to you brethren a few
religion which has sheltered and still fostering the remnant
shattered to pieces by Roman I am proud to belong to the
refuge with us in the ver their holy temple was
remnant of the Israelites southern India and took
proud to tell you that we our bosom the purest
the refugees of all religi of the earth. I am
proud to belong to a nation red the persecuted and
universal toleration, but religions as true. I am
both tolerance and univers We believe not only in
I am proud to belong to hich has taught the world
the honor of bearing to the idea of toleration.
have told you that these me ar-off nations may well claim
this platform who, referring delegates from the Orient.
all classes and sects. My thank also to some of the speakers on
thank you in the name of mi s d millions of Hindu people of
world; I thank you in the nam of the mother of religions, and I
I thank you in the name of the most ancient order of monks in th
e in response to the warm and cordial welcome which you have g
nd Brothers of America, it fills my heart with joy unsp

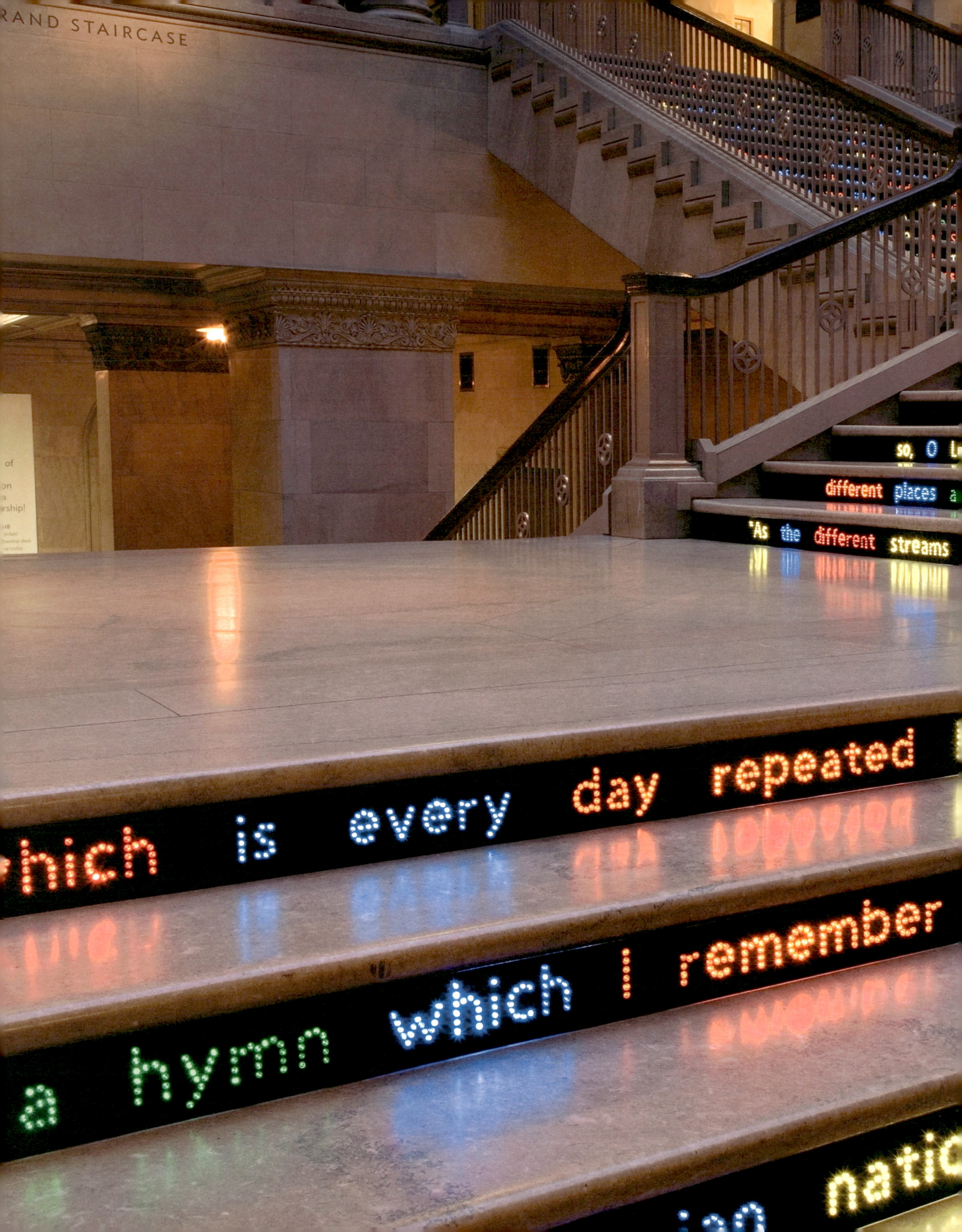
GRAND STAIRCASE
so, O L
different places
"As the different streams
which is every day repeated
which I remember
a hymn
nation

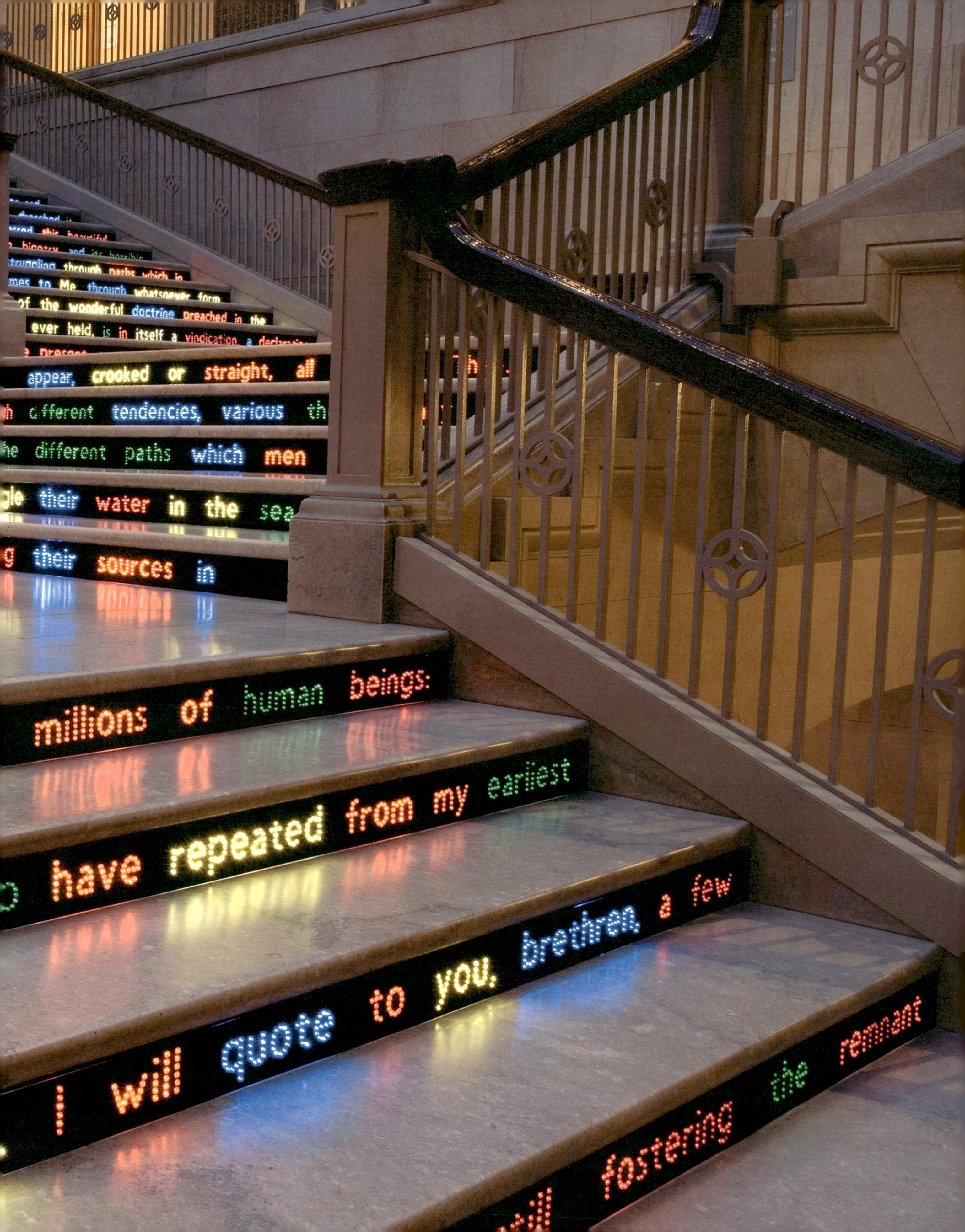

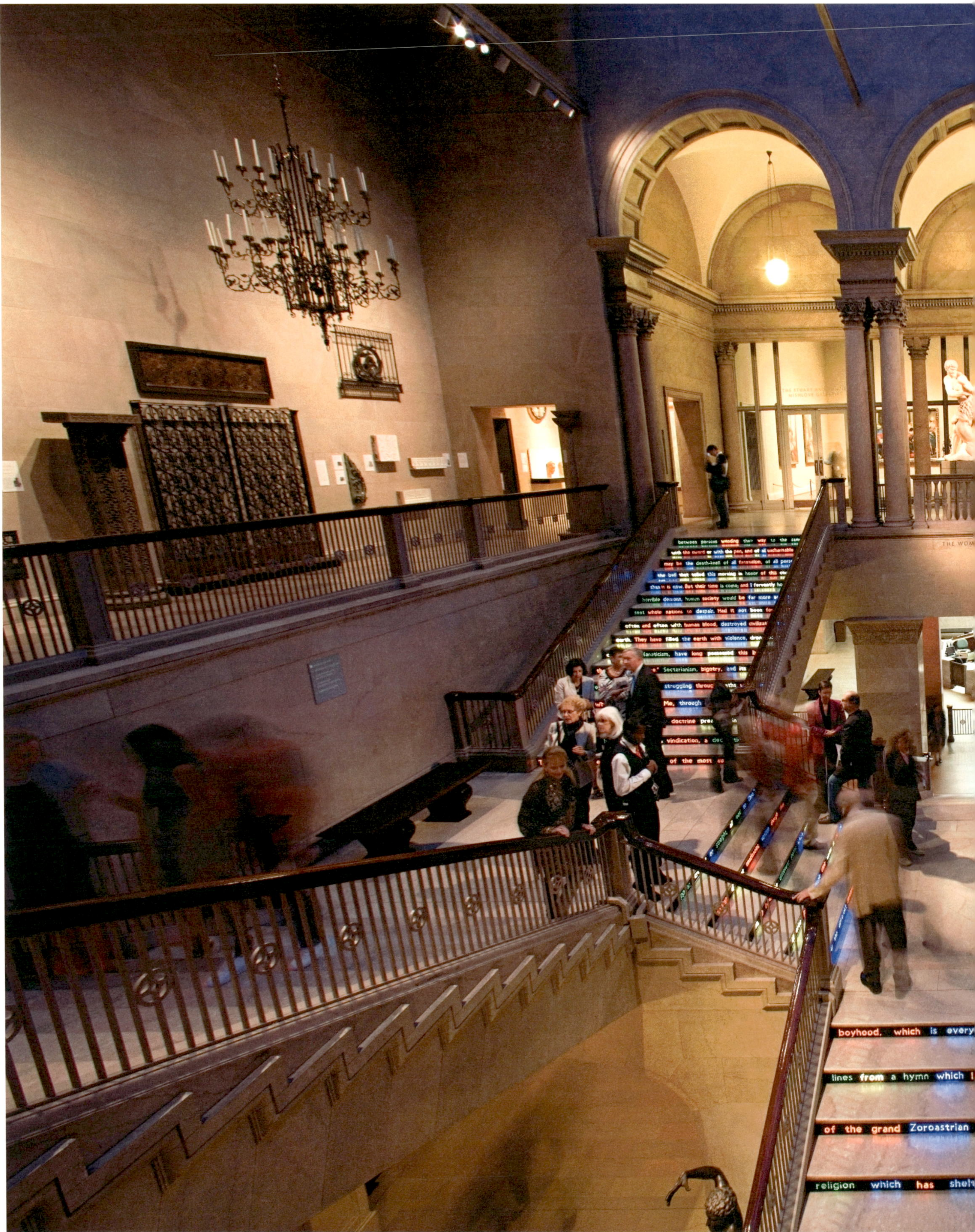

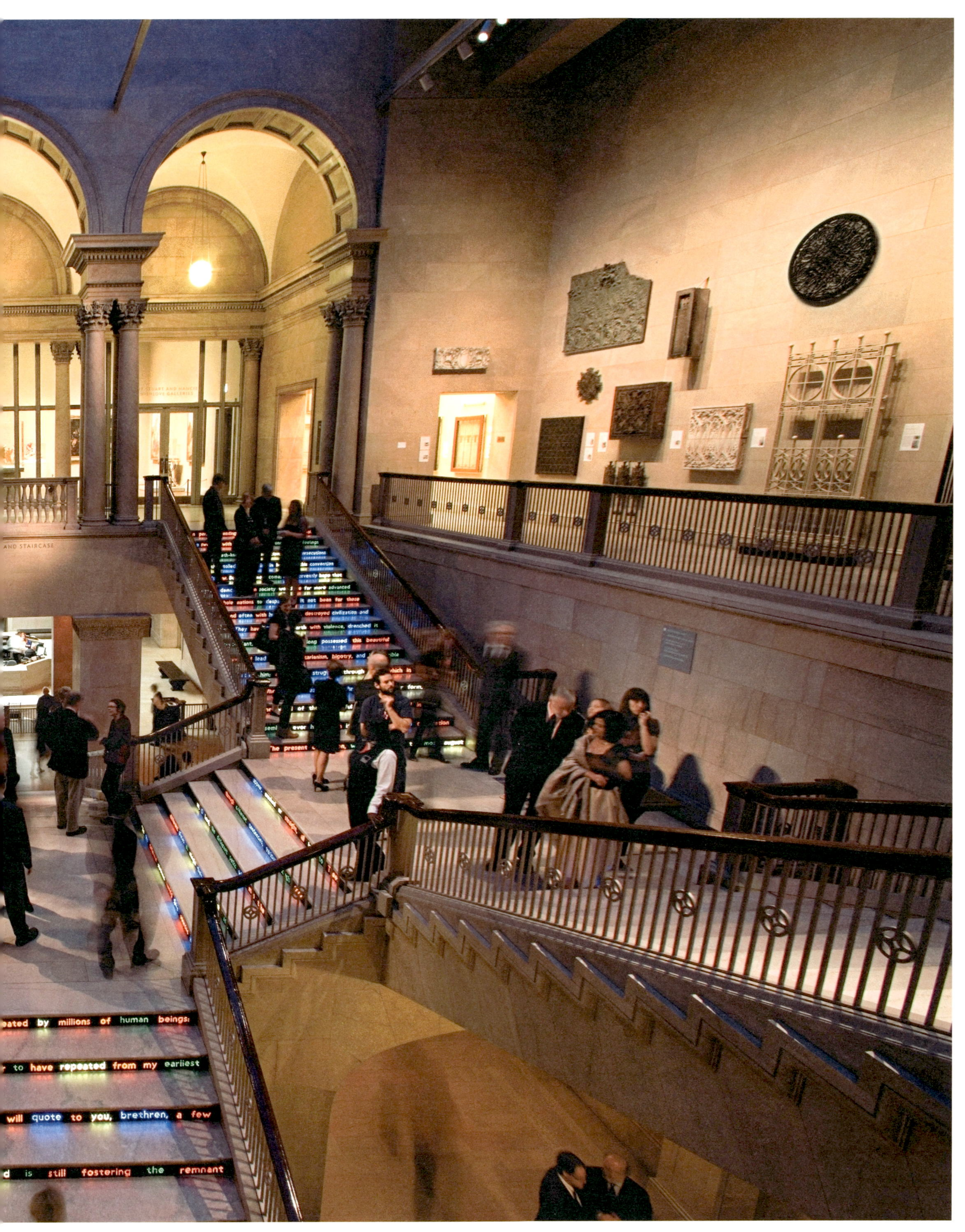
eated by millions of human beings:
r to have repeated from my earliest
will quote to you, brethren, a few
d is still fostering the remnant

Editor's note: The exchange of e-mails presented below began on Sunday morning, August 22, 2010, and included the following individuals: James Cuno, President and Eloise W. Martin Director of the Art Institute of Chicago, who was writing from Vermont while on a late-summer vacation; Jitish Kallat, corresponding from his home in Mumbai; the well-known Indian art critic Geeta Kapur, writing from her home in New Delhi; Professor Homi K. Bhabha of Harvard University, having only just returned from an extended stay in India and Italy, writing from Cambridge, Massachusetts; Jeremy Strick, Director of the Nasher Sculpture Center in Dallas and formerly director of the Museum of Contemporary Art in Los Angeles; and James Rondeau, the Art Institute's Chair and Frances and Thomas Dittmer Curator of Contemporary Art, writing from Chicago. The conversation continued intermittently throughout the coming week and concluded on August 31. —Robert V. Sharp

DAY 1: SUNDAY, AUGUST 22, 2010

JIM CUNO: Good morning/evening, everyone. I know some of you won't be participating today, and I will be traveling during some of today. But we might as well get started with whom we can.

Jitish, could you tell us when, where, and with whom you studied art and what the curriculum was? That is, as we will be discussing (in part), the character and content of national and international artistic identities. Were you (could you possibly have been) trained as an "Indian" artist? And were the political pressures of the day felt in your education, in the curriculum and classroom, among your classmates and faculty?

JITISH KALLAT: Jim, I feel that the whole act of describing oneself as an Indian artist (or for that matter as a Swedish or Korean artist based on one's place of birth or current residence) might not be a very productive enterprise. By doing so, one binds the work of art, as if one were GPS-coding its meaning to just one isolated location. At the same time, using commonly deployed terms such as "global" or "international" to describe an artist seems equally unsatisfactory, as if these were categories that bear some unanimously understood characteristics that plug easily into varying cultural contexts like a humble USB port.

My art education in the early 1990s, at the Sir J. J. School of Art, which was founded in Mumbai in 1857, offered a wide access to works of the European Renaissance and Modernism, as well as to the many artistic traditions of India and the highly engaging work from colonial India—such as that of the Company School—followed by the work of the Indian modernists and their descendants.

The art history could be described as a mix of H. W. Janson and H. H. Arnason with the likes of Ananda Coomaraswamy. I might add here that the faculty wasn't always competent or committed enough to deliver this wide basket of knowledge and that one's early intellectual development happened through confrontational exchanges with the teaching faculty and dialogue among one's peers.

My first year in art school was also the moment of India's liberalization, and the nation moved briskly from a single, state-run television channel to the sound and visual detonation of broadcast giants such as BBC, CNN, and MTV. The tentative embrace of the global and the rapid acculturation that followed were ironically paralleled by a simultaneous ascent of religious fundamentalism and the birth of a new right-wing "rioting" politics. I was eighteen then and somehow my art education hadn't prepared me to fully grasp this complex backdrop. It was only in retrospect a couple of years later that I realized how this peculiar moment—when India was trying to reach out to the world and ventilate itself culturally, only to be simultaneously held hostage by the politically stirred-up wounds of its communally volatile past—was central to my thinking about art.

Having said that, in today's hyperlinked world where inspiration and stimuli are borderless and duty-free, I feel the idea of the nation isn't any more a potent tool to comprehend artistic practice. So attaching the noun "Indian" like an adjective to describe an artist may not hold good as the syntactic precision or descriptive capability of the adjective to differentiate has dissolved somewhat in today's world, integrated though it may be by satellites in the sky and fiber-optic cables under the sea.

JIM CUNO: Thanks, Jitish. I feel much the same about the label "American." But I wonder if the legacy of political troubles during the 1980s and 1990s, with the rise of the Bharatiya Janata Party—the Indian People's Party—and the Hindu-Muslim rioting, didn't politicize the art academy the way it did, at least in part, the university. That is, the critique of the written history and theorization of Indian nationalism was much debated at this time, with the founding of the Subaltern Studies Collective.[1] And then of course, inspired by Edward Said's work on Orientalism and by certain continental philosophers and social critics, literary scholars like Homi, who will join this conversation later, began to formulate their own practice of "postcolonial critique." Clearly questions about national identity—such as, What is the true Indian national identity? What forms does it take? Who has authority to police it?—were present, perhaps everywhere present, when you were in school. No? I'm thinking of my time in high school and university in the U.S. during the late 1960s and early 1970s. That was a period when no sensitive, self-questioning student of my generation didn't ponder and even debate matters of race, civil rights, the war in Vietnam, and national identity (whether that meant, on the one hand, "my country right or wrong," or, on the other, "black nationalism"). Was this not the case when you were a student in India during the late 1980s and early 1990s? Or are you part of a post-postcolonial generation, the way some blacks in the U.S. today might consider themselves living and working in a postracial America? And if you do consider yourself a transnational artist, does that set up conflicts with some of your colleagues in India and among critics?

JEREMY STRICK: Jitish, just to follow up Jim's question, I'm wondering if within your art-school education, any imperative was expressed to make a specifically "Indian" art, however that term might have been construed, or to make work that specifically addressed Indian culture or society. Or were such considerations absent?

JITISH: You know, Jeremy, these considerations may have preoccupied the faculty, but many of us were in fact trying to avoid such essentialism as the space around us was not cohesive and static.

Instead, it was dense with productive contradictions and a dynamic interbreeding of cultural forms at a moment of rapid and abrupt social changes.

JAMES RONDEAU: Jitish, while I understand what you are saying about the limitations of labels as such, and rightly wanting to avoid the pitfalls on any sort of essentialist point of view, the work you are doing is certainly informed by specific geographical, political, and historical circumstances that are unique to India, is it not? Or are you suggesting that we need to move past such thinking? Both the actual and the rhetorical aspects of our technological and socially interconnected spaces do not fully transcend the particularities of place and national identity, do they?

JITISH: I totally agree with you, James, that aspects of my practice would be rooted in conditions specific to the subcontinent. Also very often a work I make may have elements that deny easy translation or may translate differently across borders. Perhaps you noted from my response to Jim that I am not calling the "Indian" adjective incorrect, I'm only pointing toward its inadequacy.

Likewise, I'd hesitate to easily align with dissolved categories such as "global" and "international"; I do not have a problem with any of their usage, as indeed all of these are very commonly used. None of these descriptions is false. As an artist one doesn't want to lose the interesting torsion of working in between these categories by choosing one.

JIM: And Geeta, I'd like to hear to hear your response to my comments? And Homi, was it different being at university in Britain? And how did you negotiate relations with student colleagues at "home" in Indian universities? Were the two worlds—abroad and home, university and art school—worlds apart?

RVS: The following is an early response prepared by Homi Bhabha that he had temporary problems circulating to the other participants. It was ultimately inserted here on the third day of the e-conversation.

HOMI BHABHA: Oxford was something of an oddball situation for me. In my first year I felt rather out of place, not because I felt a stranger to the country and the customs, but because, in a weird way, I discovered that I knew a certain kind of England only too well because I came from a certain kind of India. I felt that things were utterly familiar and utterly estranged. I returned to Bombay, developed a hypochondriacal illness, and missed the next term.

After living and learning in Bombay, the social milieu of Oxford felt rather provincial—and I just couldn't understand why. The libraries, the art galleries; the cinema and concerts; the dons and the scholarship—all these were "world class" at Oxford, way beyond anything available to me in Bombay. But there was something about the active hybridization of cultural practices and values in Bombay that made the city, its conversations and confluences, remarkably invigorating. Oxford seemed pallid and self-protective.

The relentless conformity of age and class crowded into a small city—exquisitely beautiful though Oxford was—made me nostalgic for the eclectic and erratic choices that Bombay offered—to those who could afford them. "High" and "low" seemed to touch somewhere in the middle, in Bombay, and then implode into the public sphere. Oxford had a certain nobility of pedagogical purpose, but seemed bland in comparison when judged at street-level.

And, Robert, what is the etiquette of intervention—how/where do I make my responses? Can I simply introduce myself into the conversation at whatever points I think I have something relevant to say or do I have to intervene incrementally, from the time at which I join the conversation, without interfering in the flow of the conversation that went before I became a part of the group. I want to avoid large, lumpish blocks of "conversation" that look like mini-essays in disguise—pedantic and heavy-handed; but, on the other hand, if I just butt in wherever I think I have something to say, I might destroy the flow of discussion and create awkward problems of transition. Do I, for instance, respond to Jim's excellent question to me after Jeremy's "follow-up question" or before? How do we preserve the back and forth of conversation—or will you do this in the editing process? As you might gather from the time of this e-mail, I am rather jet-lagged, but will get into the act later this morning.

DAY 2: MONDAY, AUGUST 23, 2010

ROBERT SHARP: Dear Homi, good morning. My first response is "jump in, the water's fine." I think you have a proper sense that this conversation is not going to be linear and that Jim's not going to be Charlie Rose (nor am I). Instead, this conversation is going to be multidimensional and overlapping, like a great polyphonic chant, if you will, with some members speaking or writing while others are catching their breath and preparing to reenter.

HOMI BHABHA: Like James, I am somewhat less persuaded than Jitish is, that the "bird's-eye view" ("satellites in the sky") or the below-ground perspective ("fiber-optic cables under the sea") creates a hyperlinked world that makes the nation obsolete, and hence irrelevant, as a framework of political intelligibility, aesthetic interpretation, or creative innovation. Nor does the description of art or literature or architecture as "Indian" or "Mexican" necessarily essentialize these forms of cultural representation. The nation-space is a profoundly complex and contradictory geopolitical reality with disjunctive social localities, diverse political and affective identifications, and differentially constellated (and articulated) communities (national and international). It is this skein of political power and civil procedure that defines—through the agency of citizenship and alienage—the democratic possibilities (or impossibilities) of state and civil society, of formal and informal public spheres. To see the nation-space as quintessentially defined—either politically or culturally—by the nation-state is to substantially narrow both its cunning capillary power and, at the same time, to radically reduce spaces of creative intervention and strategies of transgression/transformation. I am with Antonio Gramsci when he says, more or less, that to be too focused on the nation-state rather than the nation-space turns the dissenting citizen into the proverbial deer caught in the headlights—at once dazzled and blinded.

The postcolonial state, however one defines it, is an exemplary instance of this complex, multisited modern (even postmodern) form of communal life. It has a double, uncanny mode of being: the nation's sovereignty (the nation in/for itself) is always dependent on its radical, uncanny relationality—its difference from "other" nations; its built-in anxiety around minorities or dissenting "others"; fraught frontiers and recurrent border tensions; cultural displacements associated with the "invention of tradition," and historical amnesias and disavowals produced in the process of the nation's originary claim to an archaic past. Postcolonial civil societies are profoundly cosmopolitan, having weathered the incursions and impositions of "international" cultural and market forces prior to encountering their own "nationalist" moments. It would not be an overstatement to say that postcolonial societies were quasi-internationalist before they were nationalist; in fact, that is precisely Frantz Fanon's point when he argues that, despite global inequalities and injustices, it is difficult to act ethically in the national interest without taking a larger view on international well-being. South Asian nationalism has had a strong internationalist/cosmopolitan aspiration inherited from the founding fathers (Mahatma Gandhi, Jawaharlal Nehru, Mohammad Ali Jinnah, Rabindranath Tagore, Annie Besant, Bhikhaiji Cama, Sarojini Naidu, Lala Lajpat Rai, Lala Har Dayal, Sri Aurobindo, Vivekananda, etc., etc.) and extending toward the more contemporary Communist, Maoist, ecological, and feminist movements.

I don't mean to give a free pass to nationalisms—forbid the thought. How could one fail to see what happened to Fanon's Algeria at the hands of the Islamic Brotherhood; or to Gandhi and Nehru's India at the hands of Hindutva or the Shiv Sena. I am suggesting something quite different. There is, I want to argue, a cultural and political difference between the nation as the vehicle of a nationalist ideology; and nationness as a quotidian practice of governmentality: a sense of agency and belonging; the everyday identifications of citizen-subjects; the nation as a jurisdiction of ethical responsibility, civic obligation, and cultural practice. The sovereignty of the nation in the former instance may have been partially compromised by the advent of globalization, transnationalism, and, in more lethal ways, by the unilateral "preemptive" military strikes of hegemonic nations. But the nation as a jurisdiction of everyday governmental practices—political, social, aesthetic—is not to be dismissed either as actuality or as aspiration. It is this latter desire for a national presence or a homeland that drives groups to make the most remarkable political sacrifices or commit the most heinous crimes of ethnic cleansing.

What has to be acknowledged, in my view, is the powerful ambivalence that exists around the desire for the nation in the public sphere; the nation—globalization notwithstanding—is a repetition-compulsion that we cannot simply overcome. For some the "drive" toward the nation is a defense against the fear of social dislocation and political humiliation; for others it is the dream of the "imagined community." This "nation-desire" is staged variously in the diverse *habitations* of globalization.

The national self-questioning that Jim talks about—affiliation and alienation as the active, on-going condition of concerned, committed citizenship—is part of this ambivalent process. There are times of crisis or social unrest when it becomes more intense; in less turbulent moments, the process of splitting and division is less urgent for individuals or groups.

RVS: As the time differences between India and the U.S. played out, it was sometimes difficult to follow the thread.

JIM: Hi, Jitish, just keeping track. I don't think you've responded to my three recent questions: first, about politics debated while you were in school; second, how your work might be read differently by different "identity" groups within India; and third, what the political nature of the critical response to your work might be. I'll get off the identity issue quickly, but it is alive in India certainly (and, of course, sadly here as well; not to mention in France, where President Nicolas Sarkozy tried to start a national debate on what it means to be French). For you, as an artist who takes on political issues in his work, what are the tensions between the "local" and the "global"?

JITISH: The sudden rise of the right wing in the 1990s brought with it not just hostility but also monopolistic claims over religious iconography, cultural practices, and even the daily lifestyle of people. Somehow these disputes didn't have much of a bearing on a largely apolitical art-school campus that was for the most part steeped in a formalist isolation away from prevailing ideological battles and political processes.

While reading your question I was also wondering about how American cultural institutions and art schools steered through the policies of the Bush administration? Did it impact the role museums played in American civil society or your own practice and the practice of Jeremy and James as leading curators and heads of museums? I'm thinking of moments such as when the U.S. Patriot Act was formed in the fall of 2001.

JIM: There were numerous effects. Homi knows more from the university point of view, and James and Jeremy can speak from theirs, but at the least the Bush administration made it far more difficult for foreign-born students and faculty to get visas to enter the U.S. and work at or attend American universities. And certainly the Bush administration's policies and actions became the subject of academic criticism and artistic practice.

HOMI: Wasn't there some Congressional Committee that partly laid the blame of 9/11 on the rise of postcolonial studies in U.S. universities? Wasn't there a famous piece in the *New York Times* that said that the U.S. had been attacked because of all the wimpish cultural relativists running around campuses abusing the cultural capital of the Enlightenment? Was Osama bin Laden really so *au courant* with literary theory? Was that his preferred pastime while he was huddled and hidden in his post-Platonic cave in his Afghani mountain resort?

Jitish keeps suggesting that as an artist he resists the "identity" question; instead he occupies an interstitial space, one that confuses categories and classifications (to say nothing of countries and cultural origins), but he refuses to be more specific about it. Jim's question about the tension between the global and the local prompts me to ask you, Jitish, to elaborate on your statement: "[V]ery often a work I make may have elements that deny easy translation or may translate differently across borders." What do you understand by the "translation" of a work? And how would such a differential translation—somewhere in between the global and the local—reveal new territories of translational or interpretational "tension" within the semiotic or

performative structure of the work. How does the *agency* of the work disclose different modes of intervention and interpretation in varying regional or institutional localities?

GEETA KAPUR: Dear all, I am going to do exactly what Homi thinks he/we should not do, and that is to introduce a roadblock into the convivial conversation by offering a "mini-essay"—though I must say that I think of it more like an intervention that turns a conversation into an argument, to good purpose. It's very long and you will of course focus on and take what you think appropriate. The rest is for the editor to decide.

It doesn't seem useful to enter a conversation where the (American) interlocutor asks the (Indian) protagonist for an identity sketch in terms of locality/ nationality/globality; where, then, the protagonist, who is an artist-subject (before he is a citizen-subject?) ducks and dissembles his way out by saying a yes and a no. This often-repeated exercise elicits always the same results. Since the diaspora vantage within postcolonial discourse took precedence as the key trope for theorizing culture/nation, the matter of identity is so irreversibly relativized that we must in fact step beyond its threshold—and yet not into a global position where the contemporary artist can too easily survive in a default mode. Rather than ask Jitish for an introductory biography with some clue to where, in the nation-space, his points of allegiance (or alienation) might point, let us look at his already large body of work to see if his art answers the questions—in both more direct and more complex ways. There couldn't be a better point of entry than *Public Notice 3* (as also *Public Notice* and *Public Notice 2*).

Kallat uses entire (unannotated) texts of seminal speeches by three valorized figures in India's cultural-political domain. As sculptural installations, these embodied texts become a concretion of speech acts emblazoned in public memory—hence their monumental scale. Since they were delivered (1893, 1930, and 1947), these speeches have been further emblematized through formal (often bureaucratic) reiteration of India's civilizational purpose, its psychic force, its national vision. Somewhat classically in the way of memorials, these inflated "word tablets" record chosen historical moments from when the nation was not yet, or just at the threshold of becoming, a state.

Jitish could be seen to mimic a form of pedagogy resembling in scale and style the impact of state memorials: the decision to freeze and frame a moving, voice-infused speech act makes the work *less actually political.* On the other hand, the materials, processes, and technologies used in this pedagogical exercise lets the haloed vocabulary be burned, stripped down, decomposed, camouflaged. For the Indian citizen, today, these memorials would be a site to commemorate national loss, even betrayal. Kallat retrieves, then turns around, the political generated in the original, utopian speech acts by an antistate logic.

Interestingly, Kallat takes away the political once again by titling the series *Public Notice* (1, 2, 3). The "public" (in his title) is a democratic face of the political in its constitutionally guaranteed, legally formatted, aspect. With the choice of the word "notice" instead of "address," he further takes away the agential aspect of the term public and gives it an administrative ring. Does he believe the Indian public has lost its agential capacity to imbibe, interpret, and critique a rhetorical form of historical address toward contemporary purposes? Or is it, rather, that his own notion of the public is so tied to the protocols of civil society that its potential for debate and dissent is foreclosed, or compromised? Does he, by ideological default, undermine the more contestatory space of the public sphere and, beyond that, the more anarchic space of the political?

Similarly, rather than want to know if Kallat is international, global, contemporary, etc., let us again look at the language, material, and form deployed in the *Public Notice* series. All three works are textual and related, in that sense, to the uses of text in conceptual art. The difference, however, is crucial to the argument at hand. Conceptual artists' texts are individual (even autobiographical), poetic, and almost always cryptic, using semiotic conundrums of philosophy and linguistic formality of concrete poetry to suggest hidden meanings. When it *is* political, conceptual art, usually presented or published as a fragment (a sentence or a phrase), or a code, tends to deploy detected, exposed, or analyzed information in the form of abbreviated "documents" with related pedagogy.

Now, Kallat does clearly enter an art-historical terrain premised on universalist/modernist (global/transcultural) assumptions: as, for example, this spectacularized take on concrete poetry and conceptual art. But he traverses this with the weight of issues other than those that determine the logic of art history. Indeed, Kallat shifts registers to work with another kind of determination: the determined (overdetermined) ground of national consciousness that seeks to reinscribe its transcendent moments of humanity in public memory, in situ (on "home" ground) but also within global discourse. This is a very particularly Indian (and Third World) strategy adopted by artists in the wake of their navigational dexterity as world citizens: not by deterritorialization, as by taking a detour through national space, the artist hopes to offer a "message for humanity" that is, in its spectacular staging, mocking or macabre, ironical and tragic. Its ambition if not its achievement lies, I suppose, in it becoming, within an evacuated, too euphoric contemporary, a hermeneutic evocation of tradition-as-history.

By addressing in Kallat's work his own chosen use of political, public, and civil society issues in India, by drawing out the art-historical issues he signals to in twentieth-century art, we can very simply say that Kallat is an artist from India if not an Indian artist.

P.S. I have more to say on the relationship of the term public with that of population and populace—terms that apply to the main body of Kallat's work—not always successfully.

And, on another plane, I have more to say on the use of the term "terror" in Robert's initial suggestions to Jitish and us about the topics of this conversation, given that this is U.S. state department coinage (post 9/11) and turns the more historical usages like terrorist and terrorism into a state of being (American)! Relatedly, to flash the U.S. color code denoting (religious/fundamentalist) terror in and through a nineteenth-century text (naïve though it is in its claims and hopes for Hindu/India and the world) produces some irony but not a critique. Here is a gross example of the American state's infantilism and cowardice—and its abuse of an obedient citizenry: what is it that Kallat is able to do with this "instrumentalized" double-coding to expose the political grotesque of our times?

HOMI: I see just where Geeta is coming from and why she finds a certain form of interlocution somewhat limiting. However, for the purpose at hand, I think that Jim's framing questions—nation, identity, globality—are quite useful because they will most likely be the questions that most of the viewers will be carrying around in their heads as they ascend the Art Institute's Grand Staircase interrupted by the inscribed risers (fig. 1) that represent the elevated speech of a nation's incipient interpellation—"the nation was not yet, or just at the threshold of becoming, a state," as Geeta puts it. By putting these framing questions in place at the very outset of this discussion, Jim gives us the opportunity to translate, transform, or transgress the terms in which the conversation envisages its indexical issues. Indeed, it makes our alternative readings intelligible to a larger audience of readers and spectators.

I want both to acknowledge Geeta's roadblock—*all traffic stops here!*—and to negotiate around it to arrive at Jitish's work. And as for Geeta's objection to the precedence of the "artist-subject (before he is a citizen-subject?)," let me come at this from a different direction, not incompatible with Geeta's thinking. Hasn't the discourse of citizenship and the rights/representations that go with it (T. H. Marshall's classic trio: political, economic, and social rights)[2] been depleted of the whole domain

73

of second-generation cultural rights that have a postcolonial provenance? The political rationale of citizenship has been progressively depleted of the entire range of values and powers that we associate with imaginative and ethical action and, as a consequence, the realm of aesthetics as well as the domain of psychic and social *affect* have been bleached out of political rationality and the image of the effective citizen-agent.

So perhaps here, in responding to Jitish's work, we have an opportunity to conceive of the artist-subject as integrally and inherently a part of the citizen-subject; we have an opportunity to properly expand our notion of the artist-citizen by introducing, *into the concept of citizenship*, both the social and semiotic imperatives of cultural *representation*—image, digitality, narrative, figuration, web-based technologies—as well as the ethical imperatives of *affective agency*—anxiety, humiliation, terror, shame, aspiration, ambivalence, hope, courage, forbearance, survival, solidarity. How else can we understand—politically and phenomenologically—acts of martyrdom conducted at once in the name of God and the nation-state?

To conceive of the artist-citizen in this way requires us to rethink the issue of the "public" that Jitish is addressing—or *constituting*—in *Public Notice 3*. This is an issue at the heart of Geeta's critique. Jitish "takes away the political" by "*taking away* the agential aspect of the term public and gives it an administrative ring" [my emphasis]. Geeta argues that Jitish—by using the title *Public Notice* (rather than the more agential, *public address*)—preserves the formal, constitutional façade of the "political" associated with the norms of civil society, just as his work shares the formal mimetic resonances of state memorials. Does Jitish get beyond this roadblock? I am not sure; but here's a thought.

It could be argued that *Public Notice 3* does not so much address an already existing national "public"—Indian or otherwise—as it attempts to construct a cosmopolitan, transnational "public" around the totemic ideal of religious tolerance. Is this aspirational "public" anything more than an ethereal hope-in-hell floating in the mystical vapor of wishful thinking? Vivekananda's speech—Jitish's un-text—provides a much more interesting concept of an emergent, incipient "public" that

has a national-cultural location but not one that is narrowly nationalist; on the other hand, it has an elevated, metaphysical tone but one that does not reach out to a bland universalism. Why? Because Vivekananda, as an Indian/Hindu citizen-subject assumes an enunciatory position that is affiliated with—and in solidarity with—the experience of "international' minorities who have been the victims of political and religious persecution and terror.

> I am proud to belong to a nation which has sheltered the persecuted and the refugees of all religions and all nations of the earth. I am proud to tell you that we have gathered in our bosom the purest remnant of the Israelites, who came to Southern India and took refuge with us in the very year in which their holy temple was shattered to pieces by Roman tyranny. I am proud to belong to the religion which has sheltered and is still fostering the remnant of the grand Zoroastrian nation.

An *amor patriae* based on the care of the persecuted foreigner; the protection of the religious or political refugee; and an ethical identification with the displaced or diasporic Other must be distinguished from a xenophobic patriotism founded on an essentialist national identity/identification. Vivekananda's national "public" is a cosmopolitan public sphere consisting of citizens, refugees, diasporics; it is an ethical community that respects the rights and representation of minorities. Vivekananda's affective mode of address represents the voice of the citizen of one country signifying the religious and political polyphony of the wretched of the earth. This is a public sphere that cannot be identified in the simple spatial polarities of local/global for two reasons: first, the historical insight that modern national territories are often sites of global settlements and the disruption or displacements of national minorities; second, "local" and "global" as spatial norms and measures cannot track the complex, contingent ways in which national imperatives and global interests intersect in the struggle between sovereignty and solidarity.

Jitish brings something of this *Public* to our *Notice*. He returns Vivekananda's address of 1893 to Chicago in 2010. The expressivity of voice and sound is replaced by the architecture of sign and silence. The call for religious tolerance is no longer a universal value; now it is a matter of the global politics of security—a matter of life and death. But Vivekananda's original "Chicagoan" text has its own double diasporic history. It is now brought from India back to Chicago by the citizen-artist Jitish in order to make an interstitial, inscriptive installation "between the stairs" that puts us all *On Notice.* The color palette of the post-9/11 security code; the spectator's restless gaze that ascends with the grand symmetry of the staircase and then descends to read "between the lines"; the interpreter of intolerance giving notice to the various geopolitical locations of fundamentalist intolerance: Chicago/ Mumbai, etc., etc., etc. Always also the danger of the "foundational" text—Gandhi, Vivekananda— itself becoming a kind of fundamentalist utterance. Walking up the Woman's Board Grand Staircase, reading the illuminated risers, our eyes and our feet meet. Does *Public Notice 3* mourn or mimic the slow elevation of monumentality?

JIM: I also want to say, Geeta, that your comment is perfect: a meaty response to the question put to Jitish. Many thanks. May I ask does this hold true for you in your practice as a critic? Do you find yourself writing in the "in-between spaces" of the global/local practitioner, writing about art made in India/by Indian artists for an Indian audience (local and/or in the diaspora) and an international audience? That is, could what you write about Jitish be written about you as a critic of contemporary art?

JAMES: Jitish, I will try to pick up on your question a bit. It must be acknowledged that much cultural practice in the U.S. during the years of the Bush presidency remained insufficiently politicized. The work of a few, key artists and activists with a sustained commitment to political engagement began to feel urgent again, particularly among those with a committed antiwar position. Like the 1980s in some respects there was a sense that advanced artistic or intellectual pursuits were automatically aligned with a position of resistance. A somewhat insidious notion of "us vs. them" pervaded, alongside a resigned sense of pessimism. But honestly the narrative surrounding the state of the visual arts during the Bush years is really, perhaps sadly, an economic one. Market conditions, seemingly guaranteeing a never-ending cycle of price escalation, speculation, and all of the values attendant to those

conditions, were such that the art "world" became synonomous only with the art "market." The rapid acceleration, one would even say hyperinflation, of the market certainly increased the sense of divide between those validated by the marketplace and those not. The result here, it seems to me, has been the further marginalization of socially engaged art. Jitish, how has the recent, rapid expansion of the markets for contemporary Indian art affected what you are able to accomplish?

RVS: Late on Monday, Jeremy Strick, who had also been traveling, was able to weigh in again.

JEREMY: Broadly speaking, I would concur with James Rondeau's assessment. As Jim Cuno suggests, the direct impact of the response to 9/11—the wars in Afghanistan and Iraq, and the passage of the Patriot Act—was certainly felt by American museums in discrete areas such as the challenge of obtaining visas. More generally, museums eventually went about their business, feeling less effect than might be imagined given the significant changes operating both within the society and its external relations. This reflected a broader condition in which the millenarian rhetoric of a war on terror and empires of evil clashed with a consumerist injunction—defeat terror by buying— that was effectively if not necessarily intentionally followed in the art world. That and other dissonances create difficulties for the interpretation of art and of actions.

Let me offer a personal anecdote: a few days after 9/11, I wandered through the store at the Museum of Contemporary Art in Los Angeles and noticed that we had for sale a postcard of a work by John Baldessari from the museum's collection: *Two Highrises (with Disruptions)/Two Witnesses (Red and Green),* 1990. The bottom half of the work shows exploding twin towers, massive plumes of smoke intertwining from their tops. The image seemed shockingly premonitory. I called the artist and asked him about the work, and whether he was comfortable with us displaying the postcard at that time. He asked that it be temporarily removed from sale. My sense was that he felt that immediate response to this work would be too freighted by the events and images of the past few days, that its reception would be overdetermined.

That risk of overdetermination seems to me a primary challenge when inserting art or actions into an interpretive context freighted with momentous events or with complex and highly contested categories. Perhaps more so when those categories are typically formulated as binaries (local/global) between which one must choose or—in effect—be chosen.

So, I appreciate Geeta's account, both of the e-conversation itself, and of *Public Notice 3*. By that account, I imagine that *Public Notice 3* will be a particularly effective negotiation of, and commentary upon, the various powerful categories, conditions, and imperatives at play. I imagine, too, that *Public Notice 3* will deliver a fair measure of its bite from the historical specificity of its siting—that in that place, the various artistic strategies sketched out by Geeta will carry a special force.

I wonder, then, about how the questions raised in this conversation pertain to other works by Jitish—that is, to works other than *Public Notice, Public Notice 2*, and *Public Notice 3*. To the works on canvas, for example. Or to the sculpture. To work displayed at commercial galleries or in international exhibitions. To work, in other words, made less to address a specific place and history, but rather to be inserted into the market and collections, public and private, and into the context of the international exhibition which, while "global" events, nonetheless enforce ideas of national identity.

I suppose I am asking this question first of Geeta, but would welcome responses from all, including, of course, Jitish.

DAY 3: TUESDAY, AUGUST 24, 2010

JITISH: I'd like to add to what Jeremy said about trying to defeat terror by foregrounding normalcy. Ironically, going to the movies immediately after a bomb blast at a cinema hall can be a political act.

As an artist, I know that most of the time the act of making a piece and showing it is akin to publishing a doubt . . . like notations one makes within a self-addressed envelope that might travel the world but the person you are addressing is yourself. I see my practice as touching upon various types of image making—a painterly practice that might

refer at once to the format of the billboard and history painting [see fig. 2]—or sculptural works and photographic works that vary greatly in the methodology of their making and share very little formal resemblance between them, but remain tied by broad themes of sustenance, survival, mortality.

James, in spite of the many pitfalls that the expanded market threw up, one might add that in a place like India, with the absence of any enlightened state support for the arts, this has had an enabling effect. Throughout the 1970s and 1980s and up until now, a few select private galleries have continued to facilitate the staging of works that push conventions, and recently they have been empowered to do much more. In a peculiar way, following the rapid market growth and its subsequent reshuffling during the economic crisis, works of several engaged practitioners have gained prominence.

And, Homi, the satellites that suddenly became active in the early 1990s and the fiber-optic cables that were laid within years of my leaving art school altered my visual vocabulary—a bit like B.C. and A.D.: "before cable" TV and "after Doordarshan." (For those who don't know, Doordarshan is the public television broadcaster in India, and it was, for many years, our state-run, single-channel, low-intensity entertainment.) As I mentioned, this moment of India's opening up was an integral part of my artistic formation, and there was indeed a lot of TV in my early work. Perhaps I could say that television was to my early work what the city street is to my later work.

My feeling is that describing either my art practice or my art education as "Indian" will remain somewhat deficient unless broken, hyphenated, and interrupted with other words that might make this description slightly fuzzy and rippled. Used as an adjective and additionally placed in waterproof quotes, it would make the reception (the moment of the nineties, since Jim was referring to my early education) look singular and clear like HD, while in fact the vision at that moment when the nation was still tuning in, was blurred with signal overload and fractured reception.

HOMI: I appreciate what you say about the influence of 1990s liberalization and technological innovation on you and your work. I am still not convinced by your validation of the "borderless and duty-free." The metaphor doesn't confront the complexity of the global condition or the fate of the nation within it, as I have tried to argue.

On national designation/signification, I don't think you get my point. I am suggesting that most national (as opposed to nationalist) attributions of identity or history are hybrid and hyphenated. It is playing into the hands of the patriotic-purity brigade to create hysteria about "essentialism" when the national condition is, and always has been, deeply ambivalent, contingent, even cosmopolitan (particularly in the postcolonial condition).

JIM: Jitish, another question: do you think *Public Notice 3* will carry a different message in India than in the U.S.? And in India, a different message in Mumbai, Calcutta, or Delhi, and if one is an Indian Hindu or Muslim?

JITISH: Jim, as an artist I find it problematic to place a "manual of instructions" or a "manual of viewerly expectations" alongside an artwork. So I do not quite know how *Public Notice 3* might be read in India, in different cities, by diverse religious constituencies. Yet, since the individual is today formed not only by allegiance to the major categories such as nationality and religion, but also by the dispersed subscriptions one makes to a vast range of diverse stimuli, one might hypothetically wonder if two residents of the same Chicago locality, of same age, gender, education, and religious background might respond differently to *Public Notice 3,* based on, say, their orientation from the differing news channels they watch, or if they obtain their news from tabloids or broadsheets, or blogs and tweets emanating from other countries.

That said, as pieces travel they not only gather art miles, but also shed and gain meaning in collaboration with the viewers they encounter.

HOMI: I find it strange that this interesting discussion about diverse cultures of interpretation, and demographics of reception, makes no reference to the psychic or fantasmatic "reading" of the work, and its affective implications. Surely both tolerance and terror have long politico-aesthetic traditions implicating form/affect/identification that need to be explored. Does this work have no subliminal, symptomatic, or even spectral presence? Aren't these representational strategies major influences on an artist's material practice and his ability to convey meaning?

JIM: Thanks, Jitish. Yes, of course, works of art take on different meanings in different places. Here, the connection will be made with 9/11 and the response to—and *by*—the Office of Homeland Security, which has fundamentally shaped our national paranoia. In every U.S. airport, we were regularly reminded that foreign enemies were set to do us harm. And it seemed even that we could measure that threat in stages of five levels. I assume in India, the meaning will derive from a better understanding of the context of the Swami Vivekananda's speech and the historical enmity between Hindus and Muslims that has been given sharp focus since the destruction of the Babri Mosque.

JITISH: Thanks so much Jim, for your observations on the possible readings of *Public Notice 3* in the different settings of India and the U.S.

DAY 4: WEDNESDAY, AUGUST 25, 2010

RVS: Then from India, where it was already early on Wednesday, came Geeta's response to Jim and Jeremy about whether the position she assigns to Jitish as artist also applies to her as critic.

GEETA: But between Jitish and me there is a generational difference, indeed, a two-generation hiatus! I look at globalization from another historical past, in reverse perspective. Until the mid-1990s, I wrote as a Third World critic located in India geographically, and nationally. I identified with the antagonism of the Indian Marxists toward the capitalist west, and looked beyond Indian cultural practice to Brazilian, Mexican, and Cuban counterparts. I also favored the tendentious use of the term avantgarde deployed by the Cubans with such élan (and I am amused at the way the Chinese now push that term to their own purpose). Although the postcolonial turn rationalized the emphatic voice of the decolonizing world, and although changed relations between the power blocs made the Third World a largely rhetorical category, I try to find other ways to position contestatory politics in a globalized art scene.

Overleaf:
Figure 2
Jitish Kallat, *Horror-ificabilitudinitatibus,* 2009. Acrylic and glitter on canvas, bronze; 350 x 780 cm (137 13/16 x 307 1/16 in.); five bronze supports, each 53.3 x 33 x 27.9 cm (21 x 13 x 11 in). Collection of Steven Wu and Cynthia Chen, Taipei.

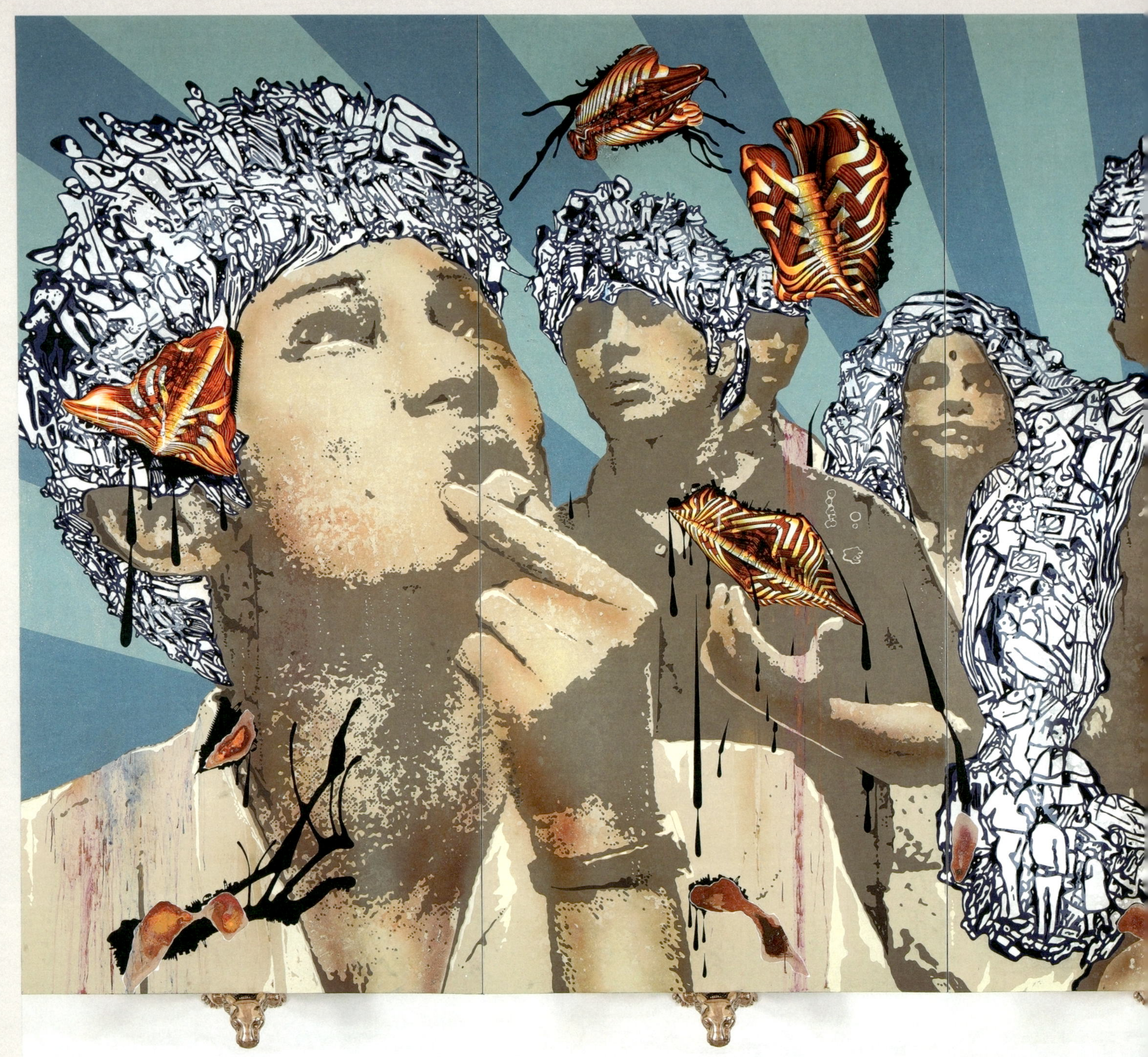

Frankly, I wouldn't accept taking up a position between the local and global; as Jeremy says, "formulated as binaries [local/global are options] between which one must choose or—in effect—be chosen." My space is still the nation-space with the criticality that it now demands, and I engage with this space (and its imaginary) as also with the *place* (for politics) that it offers. Given the irreversibility of transcultural navigation, we can't perhaps hold on to the national-international combine as in the days of socialism; but maybe the privilege of a cosmopolitanism that was *alive* with contradictions in the worldview of the Third World protagonists (or antagonists) is still an option. In any case, I resist entering the *negotiating* mode inherent in the local-global paradigm.

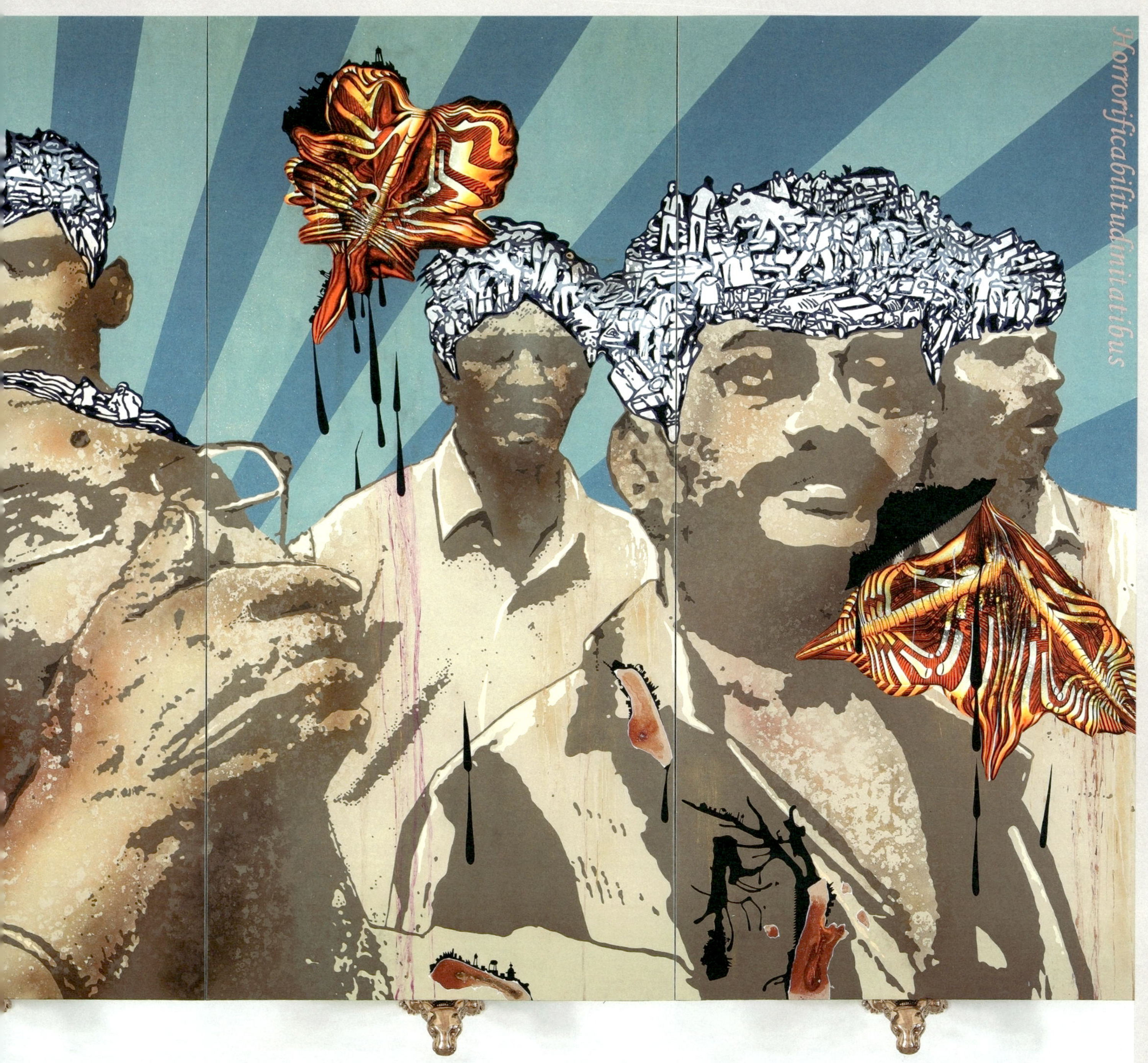

I couldn't be happier than to hear Homi say: "What has to be acknowledged, in my view, is the powerful ambivalence that exists around the desire for the nation; the nation—globalization notwithstanding—is a repetition-compulsion that we cannot simply overcome."

I doubt if Jitish and his generation speak of such desire, and their indifference extends not only to an earlier, more ideological, form of the political but, if I might say so, to the political itself or, in any case, to its emancipatory agenda within (and without) the nation. Their concerns are, indeed, different, and Jitish offers an eloquent articulation in words and work.

Interestingly, a large part of Jitish's work is a *figural representation* of social deprivation, assault, and fear, and the ground is urban India, specifically Mumbai [see fig. 2]. Proposing a multilevel reflexivity, this representation is subjected to an ironical double- (and triple-) take, that defers and displaces the "message": often for the better. But at other times it takes a strange turn: the language games he deploys, the plethora of signs he packs in, the allegories and the somewhat arbitrary referentiality to past art (e.g., history painting), all this does not offer the kind of meta-representation Jitish hopes for. This massive accretion of image-data results in something like a (semiotic) devolution.

I mention some of the problems with representation in our times, and here, in the case of Jitish, the impossible question: who one represents to whom. In the age of realism this was a well-determined position. Now, the composition of the polity—a transnational polity?—is so diversified, and the discourse around it so far complicated, that definitional security is unavailable. How, for example, is Jitish's (often) literal subject matter, how is his (often) literal form of address, positioned with regard to crucial categories: *population* (of the poor), *populace* (as governable entity), and the *people* (with agency), and a little set apart from these cumulative categories, the formal *sphere of the public*? While these concepts require a well-articulated political perspective, the very categories blur on account of Jitish's proclivity to melodrama, and representation takes a turn toward a heavily laden pathos (a hidden sentimentality? a seduction of the viewer?). This, then, is a (temperamental) retraction from the political, it might also indicate an ideological inclination toward social concern that is, in the first place, *apolitical*.

In view of the above, his Public Notice series is extraordinary in that it actually sets up and faces the issues: the (Indian) people and the (national/now global) public, and he allegories the invocation, and destruction, distortion, and/or dissolution of the relationship between these in *Public Notice, Public Notice 2,* and *Public Notice 3.*

RVS: Jim Cuno was the first to reply to Geeta on the 25th.

JIM: Thanks so much, Geeta. This is very helpful. Fascinating to read about the generational differences. There is a similar phenomenon here, between African Americans who came of age during the civil rights era, and those born a decade later and working now, not blind to discrimination but not having experienced politically enforced segregation.

HOMI: Here, I am very much on the same page as Geeta. I have little time for the "local/global" dichotomy, which is often used polemically to indicate an antagonism or to resist the sway of globalization. But the choice ends up by being too symmetrical an opposition, despite the differences in scale. Geeta and I would argue (in the company of Fanon), that to be asked to choose between the local and the global is to be faced with a univocal choice that is never free. The problem for the Third World, Fanon argued, was the binary, polarized choice offered by the Cold War. To choose socialism in such circumstances—even if that was your preferred option—could not be seen as a free and independent act.

JIM: Jitish, you might look again at my earlier questions. I'm interested in the local/global tensions in your practice (if you feel there are any) and the place that the Indian diaspora might play in your work, market, and critical reception. Also, could you remark on the theme of urban terror in your work? While locally based, it would of course have relevance and resonance in London and New York, and elsewhere.

JITISH: Here is my response to Jim's question about the tension between the "local" and the "global" in my work.

RVS: And here Jitish attached a picture of his panoramic, time-lapse photograph Artist Making Local Call *and a detail from it (figs. 3–4).*

JITISH: Jim, while thinking through your question about the tension between the local and global in my work—and while reading Geeta's richly layered formulation about generational (in)difference—I realized that I have hardly used the term "local" while talking about my work. I've often used words such as the immediate, the neighborhood, or perhaps even the city street. I am aware that they lack the intonation of the term "local" and are marked with simpler ideas of proximity, familiarity, etc. That said, I've used the word in the title of one of my photo-works, *Artist Making Local Call*, but I observed that I have never used the word "local" while talking about this work.

To describe the piece a little: for *Artist Making Local Call*, while using the format of the panorama—something that is generally used to capture a vista from the top of a hill or a skyscraper—I was taking this expansive format to the cumbersome space of the city street. The camera takes about a minute or two to complete its rotation and register a 360-degree picture, ensuring that the still photograph has that much "time" enshrined within it. The result is that an auto-rickshaw and a taxi that both happened to be in the same spot, seconds apart from each other, appear in the picture as a virtual collision. The people walking on either side of this collision are the same; they simply moved across in the time that passed. The work is thirty-four feet long and hence we might spot the same people in various places, creating a staggered march; elsewhere, people moving against the direction of the camera's rotation cast shadows while their bodies remain invisible, evoking notions of death or absence. This piece is set against the backdrop of small shops and establishments, cybercafes and food stalls, and I myself am anchored within the location of the rapidly disappearing PCO-ISD stall (i.e., public call office–international subscriber dialing). But my interest is not so much in the signifiers of the local or the contact points with the global, but the sense of an abrupt collision disrupting a simple urban march of people going to work and notions of survival and mortality.

JAMES: Jitish, I'm interested in the possible readings of this image. On one level, I see you emphatically contextualized by the space of the city, a classically cosmopolitan self-representation. But the title and the image tell us you are using an international subscriber calling station (an already nostalgic site?) to make a "local" call. Is this an ironic stance, this image of an "artist" with limited (self-limited?) horizons? I'm also curious why you used "artist" in the title. Why not identify it as a self-portrait? Do you intend to represent a more general "type" here rather than "self," strictly speaking?

RVS: On the afternoon of August 25, Jeremy responded.

JEREMY: While different audiences and individuals will always find different readings of works of art, and the artist can't expect to control those poten-

tial readings, I wonder, Jitish, if your work doesn't open up a particular space of tension or uncertainty for viewers and interpreters of your work. At the level of strategy, it seems to me the work could be equally well and in much the same way unpacked by reasonably culturally literate gallery-goers whether in Mumbai, London, or Chicago. But the subjects and their sources—whether from the Mumbai street or historically specific and resonant public addresses—call upon a different cultural literacy. Frankly, in looking at images of your paintings, or in reading Swami Vivekananda's address, I am confronted with how much I do not know about your sources and references, and the consequent inadequacy of my response. That contrasts with my comfort and sense of familiarity with the structure of your work, the various moves so well sketched out by Geeta, and creates an acute awareness that my response must necessarily be different from that of someone fluent in those sources and references. Is this a problematic inherent in the reception of any work of art, particularly as it moves from one site of reception to another, or does your work take specific measures to open up this space of tension and uncertainty?

DAY 5: THURSDAY, AUGUST 26, 2010

RVS: On the morning of August 26, Jitish sent this response to the previous day's discussion.

JITISH: Thanks so much Jim, Geeta, Jeremy, and James. Yesterday as I was reflecting on Jim's question, it made me wonder why I've instinctively used words such as the immediate. While I found several answers in Geeta's posting, I felt that sharing an image of *Artist Making Local Call* and thinking through this one piece with all of you might help raise further questions about my work or help find answers.

Referring to myself as "artist" and defining the phone-call as "local" were at once playful and deliberate choices. Given that from the calling station, one could make short or long distance calls, the title simply indicates the distance of the call I was making. (Interestingly, the phone instrument to make the international calls was placed inside the cigarette shop next to me, so this call was decidedly "local.") I felt the piece was in many ways about

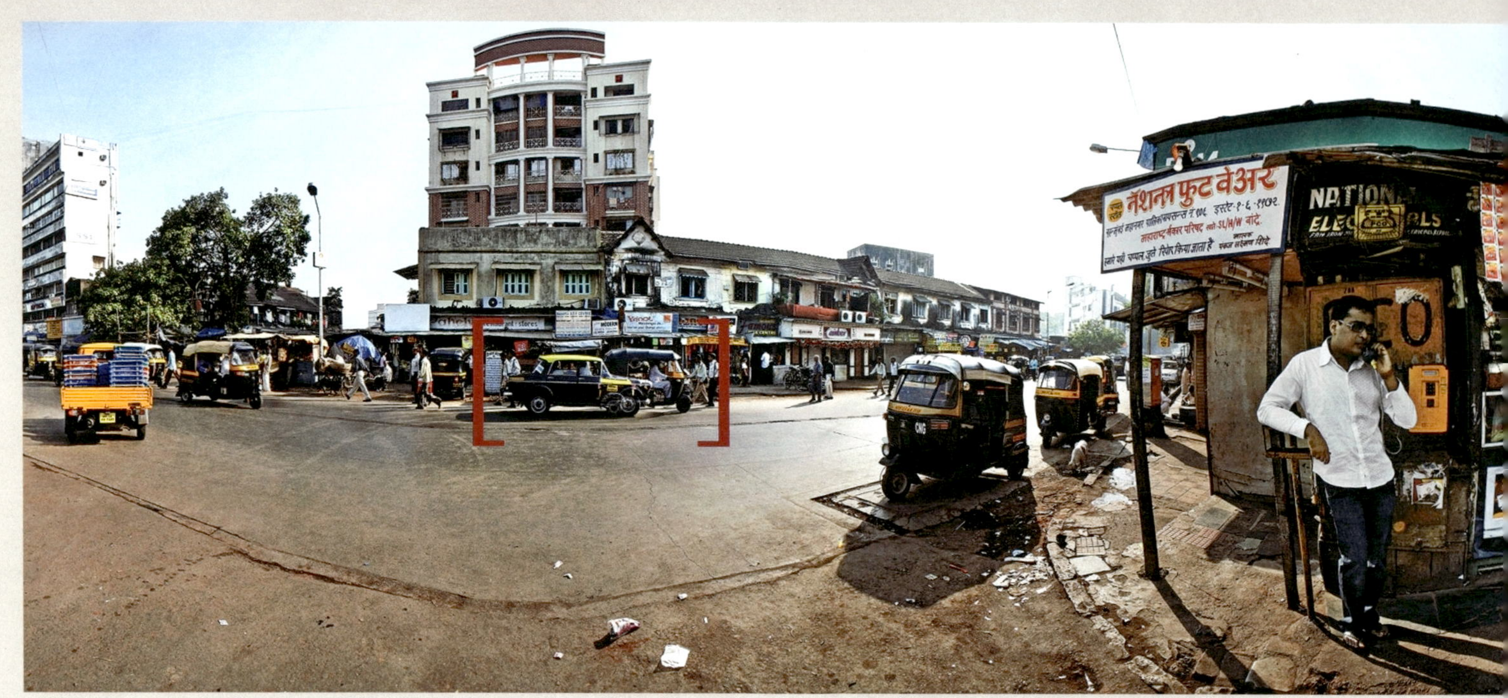

myself as an artist, ever so often having the urge to dial and make an inscription as life and death take turns to keep the world rolling.

I was also thinking of artists such as Bhupen Khakhar, Gulam Sheikh, and Sudhir Patwardhan (Geeta's peers) from whom I inherit several aspects of my practice. Perhaps if Bhupen were to visit this calling station through his painting, I wonder if he would have mischievously foregrounded the two suspended signboards "National Footwear" written in Hindi and right next to it the sign that reads "National Electricals" to drill out awkward associations and quirky insights from those simple signages. Perhaps Sudhir Patwardhan would have painted the man who runs the shop, fixing paan and selling cigarettes, while operating two telephone systems. Instead the space I occupy seems like an anomaly or a dream, where the same people march on like an apparition resembling Muybridge's movement pictures only to be disrupted by a virtual collision that never actually happened; just as the shadows on the road once had bodies that are now invisible.

Indeed, when I make a piece like this, I'm making multiple choices that are at once deliberate and arbitrary. Jeremy, while I might be subconsciously aware of some of the tensions, I don't take specific measures to ease them; I enjoy the inconsistencies and the fact that some elements remain cryptic, allowing a kind of fluctuating legibility.

DAY 6: FRIDAY, AUGUST 27, 2010

HOMI: Jitish, I don't get it. In what sense are the global or the international "dissolved categories"? In their different ways, both of them have discursive determinants, material/institutional histories, and specific political projects. In being too meticulous about being "classified" and "named," you are now in danger of a kind of artistic evaporation! I think it has become urgent for you to tell us what you understand to be your "translational location."

JITISH: My responses in this conversation, Homi, have been mostly in the context of having to choose from the following assortment of suggested options to describe myself: "Indian artist," "international artist," "global artist," "transnational artist," and "post-postcolonial." This is a hard choice to make for the many reasons that Geeta has so succinctly articulated. I might resist having to embrace voluntarily any one of these positions as conclusively accurate for the purpose; at the same time I agree that I can't wish away the fact that these categories exist and are potent (as you render each of these with so much texture); and these categories will continue to be applied to me (as they will be

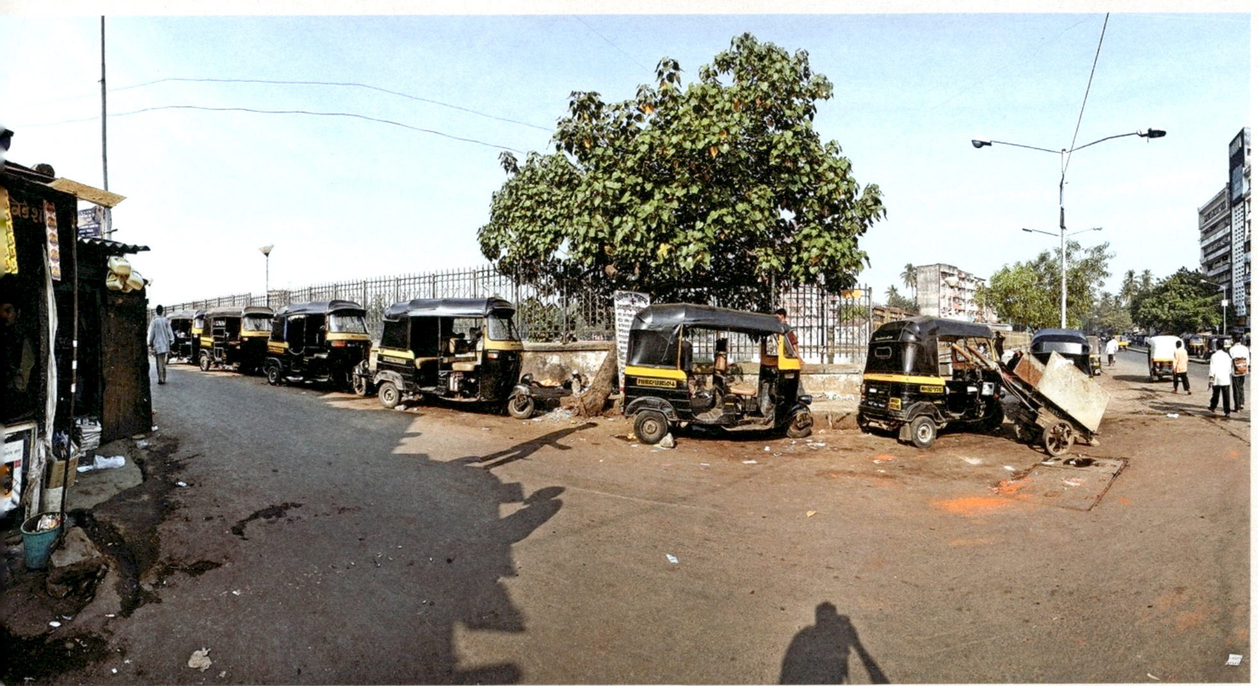

Figure 3
Jitish Kallat, *Artist Making Local Call*, 2005. Digital print on vinyl mesh; 238.8 x 1043.9 cm (94 x 411 in.). Collection of the artist.

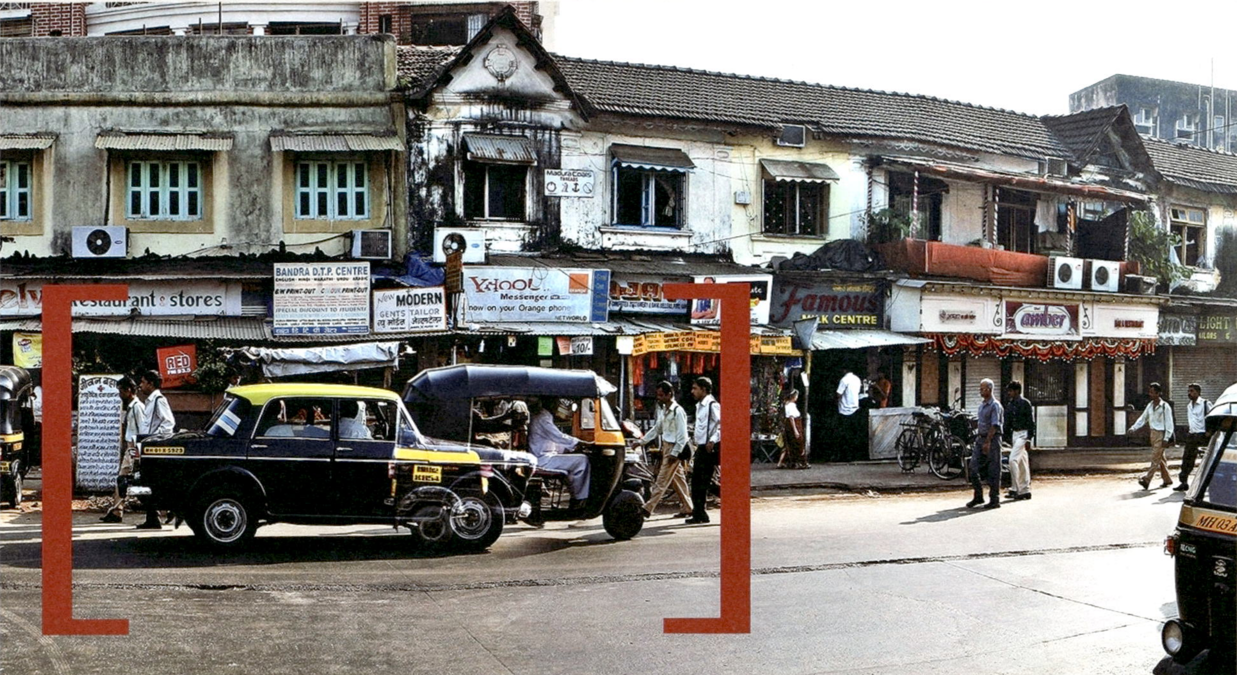

Figure 4
Artist Making Local Call (detail), 2005.

to several other artists working today). Please read my comments not as isolated evaluations of these varied terminologies but as an appeal (or a justification) for "my" need to "not-choose."

To recount what I said earlier, the term "Indian" when applied to my position as a prefix is restrictive and doesn't reflect my worldview, unless rippled by dropping in pebbles of the other categories. I find the much-used terms "global," "international," or "transnational"—if I apply these to myself— too wide and presumptuous, as if I were working within an oceanic laboratory of possibilities with unlimited access to navigational devices. Finally, you have described my noncommittal stance as being in danger of "artistic evaporation." To my own surprise, if I indeed have to commit, I find the perils in this position a useful category to be in. Since evaporation isn't the same as extinction, but is in fact a regenerative condition with the potential for movement across borderlines as a shape-shifting "cloud," as well as the possibility to condense and form puddles in unpredictable zones, I find this prospect rather exciting.

DAY 7: SATURDAY, AUGUST 28, 2010

HOMI: A nice riff off the metaphor! But, Jitish, it surprises me how you repeatedly misunderstand questions that relate to the practice and positionality of your artwork—its angle of vision, the location of its address—and misrepresent them as restrictive demands for the categorization or classification of the persona of the artist. It is you who place your practice within a hyperlinked world that is borderless and duty-free; it is you who talk about "productive contradictions" and "dynamic interbreeding of cultural forms at a moment of rapid and abrupt social changes"; it is you who propose the translational location somewhere in-between national, regional, and global dynamics; it is you who refer to the obsolesence of the nation-form. This is to say that you are well aware of the importance of such frameworks or groundworks for any discussion of your practice. But when one tries to put pressure on your terms, *in your own terms,* you somehow retreat into the protection of the artist's persona, or complain about the imposition of choices, etc.—issues that are quite distinct from the positionality of the practice (for want of a better phrase). This is not a name-game; I didn't ask *you* to embrace a position. I wanted you to talk about the positionality of your *practice.* To keep turning position into persona leads to what Geeta has repeatedly described as a turning away from politics—and, I would add, a turning away from aesthetics and ethics, too. You absolutely don't need to be the interpreter of your own work. But since you repeatedly refer to its conditions of representation, it would be illuminating to have you embrace that problem with a certain precision.

Above, I have provided a reading of *Public Notice 3.* The photographs I saw of the impressive trial installation at the Art Institute made me reflect, once again, on the way in which the work articulates an aspirational, emergent public sphere, at once national and international, that is as germane to the late nineteenth century as it is to the early twenty-first century. Written on the risers of the grandest and most public space in the Art Institute, Vivekananda's sacred call to tolerance is now reinscribed (translated) into the color-coded discourse of security. There is a kind of reverse diasporic dynamic that animates the work. A discourse on tolerance, initially delivered in Chicago via India, is now being restaged in Chicago with a double target in mind: U.S. exceptionalism and its pre-emptive war on terror; and the intolerance of Hindutva as winessed in events such as the [1992 destruction of the] Babri Mosque, and [the February 2002] Gujarat riots. This ricochet effect disrupts our sense of "local and global" as predesignated geopolitical spaces. All this I find intriguing and impressive. But when you portray your *stance* "as a shape-shifting 'cloud' as well as the possibility to condense and form puddles in unpredictable zones," I wonder whether metaphor and trope are not being manipulated in the interest of a certain mawkish evasiveness—in this conversation, at least? Am I being seduced by the melodrama, pathos, and sentimentality that, in Geeta's estimation, renders the work apolitical? I very much hope not!

DAY 8: SUNDAY, AUGUST 29, 2010

JITISH: The metaphor of evaporation to me formed an interesting conduit between earth and sky, about taking form and shifting form, and its movement across borderlines, and political and artistic fault lines—how does one move from the political to the autobiographical; does one clear one's throat in mid-utterance? Homi, these questions engage me and so the choice of the regenerative, indeterminate position was one that allowed me to imaginatively embrace many contradictions.

I'm often uncertain about the actual location of the "political." While picking a weapon, even if as an act of preemption, one has to take a firm stance, as it is all about accuracy; by contrast, the artist who receives a premonition oftentimes does so while napping. I'm thinking of the beautiful John Baldessari anecdote that Jeremy shared; also about

John's decision to withdraw the image he cast a decade ago, knowing that the passage of time has layered that piece with debris. The decision to withdraw the image off the LA MOCA shelf had to also be a retreat that John would have made to rethink the decade. Jeremy's anecdote made me think of the individual who consciously watches a movie immediately after a terror strike at the cinema and another who holds a protest placard condemning the attack outside that very building. Which of these acts is political? I don't have a firm answer; but the few options available to a citizen after such an attack also confront an artist. Rather than overdeliberate about the posture I'm taking, or the firmness of my stance, I might as well engage with the multitude of signs that travel on tiny splinters of the everyday, at once festooning and polluting our worldview.

HOMI: As I have said explicitly throughout this conversation: I am not going after Jitish's intentions at all. I want him merely to illustrate further his views of the world in which he works and the positionality he assumes in taking up a particular practice. My questions emerge from the generalizations he offers of the contemporary state of the world and the dynamics that drive it. I only want him to reflect on his own stated views of the world in which he and his artwork are inserted. This is the starting point of my questions; it is not intentionality that concerns me at all—only positionality. In a way, I want to lead Jitish away from his work in the direction of what lies around or athwart the artwork. Geeta is absolutely right: the way back to Jitish's object then becomes our project as critics or curators—not his. My question is this: Jitish, through the creative act of poesis or "making," what do you make of the world around you?

JITISH: Dear all, I'll respond with thoughts on *Public Notice 3* later this eve. Reena sadly missed her plane from Sydney due to an error in her flight booking and will be here tomorrow night instead; and our son, who's been ill, is already looking better. So I'll get back to the conversation later in the evening. Sorry about the delays since yesterday. With warm wishes to all, Jitish.

HOMI: Thanks, Jitish. I don't think I have anything to add unless Robert needs some clarification; or anybody else wants to respond. Thanks.

DAY 9: MONDAY, AUGUST 30, 2010

GEETA: Homi and Jitish, I had started writing the following, before I read Homi's "last post," so I've decided now to combine the before and after as my "last post" in this dialogue. As expected, Homi's terrifically pitched intervention in the dialogue opens out into the most important debates of our times. Many of these debates have been initiated from the very position of the citizen-subject within societies transiting from colonialism to constituted polities of new nations in the postcolonial phase— and thence into the globalizing age. It is hard on Jitish (approximately the third generation after midnight's children) to be weighed down by this historical chronology and the cumulative "roles" it spells out.

Yet, I too was troubled when Jitish resorted to so many makeovers, and took easy recourse to image-metaphors, as for example by playing on Homi's idea of "artistic evaporation." He thereby dodged what Homi calls *positionality,* and what I called *the political* and the agential role these demand. I was troubled especially because Jitish is not a shape-changing trickster. Neither his artworks nor his desire to articulate around them suggests that. On the contrary, there is, as I said before, something like an updated version of realist-melodramatic representationalism in his work that demands more determinate "answers."

This includes non-representational/"conceptual" works, like *Public Notice, Public Notice 2,* and *Public Notice 3,* where Jitish works through eminently historical subject matter; he further materializes the speech of the specters (the savants and heroes he quotes verbatim) so heavily that he almost as if "shackles" interpretative moves by the weight of the form itself. (Thus, when Homi wonders why we are not considering "the psychic or fantasmatic 'reading' of the work, and its affective implications. . . . Does this work have no subliminal, symptomatic, or even spectral presence?" my response is that Jitish's *overall* aesthetic of excess precludes the deposit of subliminal residue.) Indeed, these textual objects, this monumental installation project, is so ambitious, so evocative, so laborious, that it may (almost) exempt him from further responsibility. It is perhaps in this sense that he relies on the alibi gained simply by virtue of being a *contemporary* artist—which, as we know, is now a much valorized and audaciously self-sustaining category in itself.

On another plane, I would have so liked Homi to have enlightened us about how the domain of the public (sphere) that he brings up with reference to Jitish's work, translates into the *present political* (that I bring up). Indeed, whether he thinks this demand is valid or necessary. I am thinking of the distinction Partha Chatterjee makes between civil and political society: would Homi think that the extent of politicality that one may expect of an artist (as also I suppose of the intellectual) is finally only affective or operational within the terms of a civil society framework?[3] In other words, what is *the political* in current discourse, how does an artist engage with that, and, further in this context, how can an artist *in and from India* (no matter Jitish's many self-protecting caveats) fulfill the demands of the political, as Homi might define it.

If this is too far afield and beyond the scope of this dialogue, then I believe we must exempt Jitish from pitching into it beyond this point. I do think it extremely courageous of Jitish to enter this dialogue at all (few artists would agree to it). I also think that we may be making the mistake (presuming precisely on Jitish's articulation), of asking him to spell out his *intentions.* I imagine we are normally wary of deploying the artist's stated intention as a means for seeking/attributing meaning to an artwork. We don't ask the artist to testify to his intentions over and beyond the work at hand; instead, we interpret, speculate on, and critique meanings through theories and tropes that are, as it were, *our* (i.e., critics' or theorists') privileged domain.

DAY 10: TUESDAY, AUGUST 31, 2010

 Dear Geeta and Homi, thanks so much for your closely considered ideas about *Public Notice 3*, to which I might also append some of my thoughts.

Before that, I feel I must say that I relied on contingent image-metaphors while thinking through Homi's densely layered and perceptive interventions only to stay within the scope of my primary tool, which is "imagery." For instance, my reference to the cloud (which I inferred from Homi's idea about evaporation) wasn't really about the trickery in shape shifting, which as Geeta alerts me is neither my intention nor my format of address. While I was primarily thinking of the "cloud" in the sky (flexibility, unpredictability, mobility, forecast), I was also thinking of today's notions of "cloud computing," whose characteristics of networked interfaces, device and location independence, and co-creation with diverse sources, etc., interestingly correspond with current artistic processes.

For instance, as *Public Notice 3* takes up tenancy on the risers of the Art Institute's Grand Staircase, it draws at once on the memory inscribed within the architecture of the museum building (*site*) and commences its engagement with the public by evoking recent memories enshrined within 9/11 (*date*). It perhaps travels back through the history of the "site" to evoke yet another date, that of the World's Parliament of Religions, which was the first attempt to create a global convergence of faiths (not nations)—possibly with the knowledge that in the future it will not "only" be nations that become sole-commissioners of carnage—and overlaying these contrasting moments like an palimpsest. Swami Vivekananda's speech is illuminated, conceptually and actually, in the threat coding system of the U.S. Department of Homeland Security. I find it interesting how the advisory system co-opts five colors from a visual artist's toolbox into the rhetoric of terror, by framing them as devices to meter and broadcast threat (much like its predecessors, the British "bikini alert state" and the French "vigipirate"). The 118 risers of the museum's staircase receive this refracted text, in the "interstitial," "between the steps" as Homi interestingly puts it, together forming the experiential and contemplative transit space of *Public Notice 3*; the text is doubled at the two entry points on the lower levels of the Grand Staircase and quadrupled at the four exit points at the top, multiplying like a visual echo.

Homi brings forth a key point about the dangers of the "foundational" text itself becoming a kind of "fundamentalist utterance." I might add that nowhere is it truer than with Vivekananda's own disputed legacy and how his utterances at the close of the nineteenth century have been actively co-opted by the Hindutva brigade. In 2004, when I first invoked this speech in a piece titled *Detergent* that was shown in a gallery show in Chicago, I used the process of burning each alphabet on a mirror, a method that I had first used in *Public Notice*—with Nehru's midnight address—as if creating an internal dialogue between these two works, through the common process of incineration and shared references to the fratricidal conflicts of Babri Mosque and Godhra, among others.

Finally, I might sign off by reposting Homi's words as I couldn't phrase it better "The call for religious tolerance is no longer a universal value; now it is a matter of the global politics of security—a matter of life and death."

RVS: That afternoon, first Homi, then Geeta, replied.

HOMI: Thanks, dear Jitish, for your careful attention to all that was addressed to you. I have learned a great deal from this conversation and am delighted that its meandering form resisted the instant messaging that is the method of e-mail. I am glad we took our time. I have no further comment. Thanks everybody.

GEETA: Thank you, Homi, for making time and continuing this for the whole week. I was riveted as always by your swift, high-spirited articulation, but enjoyed it all the more as we were actually in dialogue.

Jitish, your bold, brave, reflexive responses make this project worthwhile.

And thank you all, especially at Chicago, for the opportunity.

RVS: Jim began the final wrap up.

JIM: Yes, indeed, thank all of you, especially Geeta, Homi, and Jitish, for your honest exchanges across borders (political, cultural, gender, and age). And thank you, James and Jeremy, for your intelligent and at times poignant interventions.

I very much liked the exchange format. It has the character of a real conversation. Thanks for your time and patience, all of you. As Robert said, we believe we have something memorable here. All best, and I trust your wife is home and your son is feeling much better, Jitish.

JITISH: Dear Jim, James, Jeremy, Homi, and Geeta: Thanks so much for engaging so closely with the work and for prodding me to think and focus; there is so much I've learned from each one of you in the course of the last seven days.

Reena returned late last night after a twenty-four-hour extra stay in Sydney due to her flight issue, but our son was already better since yesterday afternoon. He has eaten well since and it looks like his tummy has now settled. He resumes school tomorrow and is thrilled, as he has to go dressed like Lord Krishna. And the girls will come dressed as Radha.

Thanks once again for all that you've given me. Much affection, Jitish.

NOTES

1. The bibliography of Subaltern Studies is vast, but one could begin with the twelve volumes of *Subaltern Studies* published between 1982 and 2005 (through the agency of various editors and publishers), or with the selected anthologies drawn from those volumes that appeared in 1988, 1997, and 2001.

2. See T. H. Marshall, *Citizenship and Social Class, and Other Essays* (Cambridge University Press, 1950).

3. See Partha Chatterjee, *The Politics of the Governed: Popular Politics in Most of the World* (Columbia University Press, 2004).

SOLO EXHIBITIONS

2011

Fieldnotes: tomorrow was here yesterday, Dr. Bhau Daji Lad Museum, Mumbai. Curator: Tasneem Mehta

Stations of a Pause, Chemould Prescott Gallery, Mumbai

2010

Likewise, Arndt, Berlin

Jitish Kallat: Public Notice 3, The Art Institute of Chicago. Curator: Madhuvanti Ghose (cat.)

The Astronomy of the Subway, Haunch of Venison, London. Curator: Nina Miall

2008

Aquasaurus, Sherman Contemporary Art Foundation, Sydney (catalogue edited by Laura Cree Murray, with text by Deeksha Nath)

Skinside Outside, Arario Gallery, Seoul (catalogue edited by Jihyang Park and Kyungmin Do)

Public Notice 2, Bodhi Art Singapore (catalogue text by Shaheen Merali)

Universal Recipient, Haunch of Venison, Zurich (catalogue texts by Peter Nagy and Patricia Ellis, with interview by Nina Miall)

2007

Sweatopia, Gallery Chemould and Bodhi Art Gallery, Mumbai

Unclaimed Baggage, Albion Gallery, London (catalogue edited by Matt Price, with text by Girish Shahane)

365 Lives, Arario Gallery, Beijing (catalogue text by Deepak Ananth, with interview by Huang Du)

Rickshawpolis 3, Gallery Barry Keldoulis, Sydney (cat.)

2006

Rickshawpolis 2, Spazio Piazza Sempione, Milan (cat.)

2005

Rickshawpolis 1, Nature Morte, New Delhi (catalogue edited by Peter Nagy, with text by Deepak Ananth)[1]

Panic Acid, Bodhi Art, Singapore (catalogue edited by Peter Nagy)

Humiliation Tax, Gallery Chemould, Mumbai (cat.)

2004

The Lie of the Land, Walsh Gallery, Chicago (cat.)[2]

2002

First Information Report, Bose Pacia Modern, New York (catalogue text by Ranjit Hoskote)

2001

Milk Route, India Habitat Center, New Delhi, and Gallery Chemould, Mumbai (cat.)

General Essential, Sakshi Gallery, Bangalore (catalogue text by Ranjit Hoskote)

2000

Ibid., Gallery Chemould, Mumbai (catalogue text by Ranjit Hoskote)

1999

Private Limited-I, Bose Pacia Modern, New York (catalogue text by Peter Nagy)

Private Limited-II, Apparao Gallery, Chennai

1998

Apostrophe, India Habitat Center, New Delhi, and Gallery Chemould, Mumbai (cat.)

1997

P.T.O., Gallery Chemould and Prithvi Gallery, Mumbai (catalogue text by Ranjit Hoskote)

1. The exhibitions *Rickshawpolis 1, Rickshawpolis 2,* and *Rickshawpolis 3* are covered in the same catalogue: *Rickshawpolis* (Nature Morte and Bose Pacia, New Delhi and New York, 2007.)

2. *The Lie of the Land* and *Humiliation Tax* share the same catalogue: *Jitish Kallat: Chicago, Mumbai; The Lie of the Land; Humiliation Tax* (Walsh Gallery, Chicago, and Gallery Chemould, Mumbai, 2004).

GROUP EXHIBITIONS

2011

Maximum India, John F. Kennedy Center for the Performing Arts, Washington, D.C. (cat.)

Watercolour, Tate Britain, London (cat.)

Indian Highway IV, Musée d'art Contemporain de Lyon. Curators: Thierry Raspail, Hans Ulrich Obrist, Julia Peyton Jones, and Gunnar Kvaran (cat.)

2010

Skulptur i Pilane, Pilane Heritage Society, Klövedal, Sweden

Metropolis, The New Art Gallery, Walsall, U.K.

Indian Highway, Herning Kunstmuseum, Denmark

Changing the World, Arndt, Berlin

Urban Manners 2, SESC Pompeia, Sao Paulo. Curator: Adelina von Fürstenburg

The Empire Strikes Back: Indian Art Today, Saatchi Gallery, London (cat.)

Bring Me a Lion: An Exhibition of Contemporary Indian Art, Cecille R. Hunt Gallery, Webster University, St. Louis

2009

Indian Narrative in the 21st Century: Between Memory and History, Casa Asia Center, Madrid

Art Foundation Mallorca Collection, Centro Cultural Andratx–CCA, Andratx

All That Is Solid Melts into Air: Indian Contemporary Art in Global Times, Lakeeren, Mumbai

India Contemporary, GEM Museum of Contemporary Art, The Hague (cat.)

Mythologies, Haunch of Venison, London (cat.)

Inaugural Show, Sakshi Gallery, Taipei, Taiwan

Indian Highway, Astrup Fearnley Museum of Modern Art, Oslo. Curators: Hans Ulrich Obrist, Julia Peyton Jones, and Gunnar Kvaran

Chalo! India: A New Era of Indian Art, Essl Museum, Klosterneuburg/ Vienna (cat.)

2008

GSK Contemporary, Royal Academy of Arts, London

Farewell to Post-Colonialism: The Third Guangzhou Triennial, Guangdong Museum of Art, Guangzhou, China. Curators: Sarat Maharaj, Gao Shiming, and Chang Tsong-Zung (cat.)

Body Chatter: An Exhibition of Contemporary Indian Art, Walsh Gallery, Chicago

Indian Highway, Serpentine Gallery, London (cat.) Curators: Hans Ulrich Obrist, Julia Peyton Jones, and Gunnar Kvaran (cat.)

India Moderna, IVAM (Institut Valencia d'Art Modern), Valencia, Spain. Curator: Juan Guardiola

The Tropics: Views from the Middle of the Globe, Martin-Gropius-Bau, Berlin. Curators: Alfons Hug, Peter Junge, and Viola König (cat.)

Chalo! India: A New Era of Indian Art, Mori Art Museum, Tokyo (cat.)

Everywhere Is War (and Rumors of War), Bodhi Art, Mumbai. Curator: Shaheen Merali (cat.)

Frontline: Notations from the Contemporary Indian Urban, Bodhi Art, Berlin. Curator: Shaheen Merali

2007

Best of Artists, ShContemporary, Shanghai. Curator: Pierre Huber

Passage to India, Initial Access Frank Cohen Collection, Wolverhampton, U.K.

Soft Power, Zendai Museum of Modern Art, Shanghai. Curators: Shen Qibin, Binghui Huangfu, and Biljana Ciric (cat.)

Mad Love—Young Art in Danish Private Collections, ARKEN Museum for Moderne Kunst, Copenhagen

Urban Manners, Milan: Hangar Bicocca. Curator: Adelina von Fürstenburg (cat.)

Hungry God, Art Gallery of Ontario, Toronto

India Now: Contemporary Indian Art between Continuity and Transformation, Provincia di Milano. Curator: Daniella Palazzoli

Aftershock: Conflict, Violence, and Resolution in Contemporary Art, Sainsbury Centre for Visual Arts, Norwich (cat.)

Horn Please: Narratives in Contemporary Indian Art, Kunstmuseum Bern; Hatje Cantz, Ostfildern, Germany. Curators: Bernhard Fibicher and Suman Gopinath (cat.)

Asian Europe Meditation, National Museum of Poland, Pozan; Zendai Museum of Modern Art, Shanghai. Curator: Binghui Huangfu (cat.)

New Narratives: Contemporary Art from India, Chicago Cultural Center. Curator: Betty Seid

Thermocline of Art: New Asian Waves, ZKM, Center for Art and Media, Karlsruhe; Hatje Cantz, Ostfildern, Germany. Curators: Gregor Jansen, Wonil Rhee, and Peter Weibel (cat.)

India: Public Places, Private Spaces: Contemporary Photography and Video Art. Newark Museum, New Jersey (cat.)

2006

The 5th Asia-Pacific Triennial of Contemporary Art, Queensland Art Gallery and Gallery of Modern Art, Brisbane, Australia (cat.)

Passages, Palais des Beaux-Arts, Brussels (cat.)

Lille 3000, Lille, France. Curator: Caroline Naphegyi (cat.)

The 6th Gwangju Biennale, Korea (cat.)

Hungry God: Indian Contemporary Art, Arario Gallery, Beijing, and Busan Museum, Korea (cat.)

Made by Indians: L'Art à la Plage, Galerie Enrico Navarra, Ramatuelle, France (cat.)

Another Worlds, Arario Gallery, Cheonan, Korea

2005

Indian Summer, Ecole Nationale Supérieure des Beaux-Arts, Paris. Curators: Deepak Ananth and Henry-Claude Cousseau (cat.)

The Artist Lives and Works in Baroda/ Bombay/Calcutta/Mysore/Rotterdam/ Trivandrum, House of World Cultures, Berlin (cat.)

1st Pocheon Asian Art Triennale, Pocheon, Korea. Curator: Jin Sup Yoon (cat.)

Paths of Progression, Singapore Tyler Print Institute (cat.)

Mom and Pop Art, Walsh Gallery, Chicago

International Painting, Gallery GBK, Sydney

Kunst En Oorlod, Kunst en Cultuur Noord-Holland

Are we like this only?, organized by Vadehra Art Gallery, Rabindra Bhavan, New Delhi

2004

The Sacrifice—An Intimate I, Collection of Henri Swagemakers, Museum De Beyerd, Holland

Contemporary Art from India, Thomas Erben Gallery, New York

Summer Show, Bose Pacia Gallery, New York

Masala, William Benton Museum of Art at the University of Connecticut, Storrs (catalogue edited by Kathryn Meyers)

Zoom! Art in Contemporary India, Culturgest, Lisbon. Curators: Nancy Adajania and Luís Serpa (cat.)

Anticipations, organized by the Fine Art Resource, Jehangir Art Gallery, Mumbai

Bombay X 17, Kashi Art Gallery, Cochin

2003

SubTerrain: Artists Dig the Contemporary, House of World Cultures, Berlin. Curator: Geeta Kapur (cat.)

Drawing Conclusions: Work by Artist-Critics, New York Arts Magazine Gallery, New York. Curators: Jill Conner and Gae Savannah

Pictorial Transformations, National Art Gallery, Kuala Lumpur, Malaysia

Urban Graffiti, Woolff Gallery, London

Crossing Generations: diVERGE. Gallery Chemould's 40th Anniversary, National Gallery of Modern Art, Mumbai. Curators: Geeta Kapur and Chaitanya Sambrani (cat.)

Indians + Cowboys, Gallery 4a, Sydney. Curators: Aaron Seeto and Ruth Watson (cat.)

The Tree from the Seed, Henie Onstad Kunstsenter, Høvikodden, Norway. Curator: Gavin Jantjes (cat.)

Highlights, Sakshi Gallery, Mumbai

Hard Copy, a two-person show with Reena Saini Kallat, Gallery 88, Calcutta (cat.)

Tiranga, India Habitat Center, New Delhi. Curator: Peter Nagy (cat.)

Rain, Sakshi Art Galley, Mumbai

2002

Under Construction, The Japan Foundation Asia Center, Tokyo. Curator: Ranjit Hoskote (cat.)

India—Contemporary Art from Northeastern Private Collections, Jane Voorhees Zimmerli Art Museum, New Brunswick, New Jersey (cat.)

Clicking into Place, Sakshi Gallery, Mumbai. Curator: Ranjit Hoskote (cat.)

Glue, Gallery Sumukha, Bangalore. Curator: Peter Nagy (cat.)

Perspectiva, organized by Gallery 88, Rossi and Rossi Gallery, London. Curator: Arun Ghosh

2001

Century City: Art and Culture in the Modern Metropolis, Tate Modern, London. Curators: Geeta Kapur and Ashish Rajadhyaksha (cat.)

Indian Painting, Art Gallery of New South Wales, Sydney. Curator: Haema Sivanesan

Indian Contemporary Fine Arts, Seven Degrees and Saffronart.com, Laguna Beach, California (cat.)

Finding the Margins at the Center, Apparao Galleries, IGNCA, New Delhi

2000

7th Havana Biennial, Cuba. Curator: Hilda Maria Rodriguez (cat.)

Family Resemblances, Birla Academy of Art and Culture, Mumbai. Curator: Ranjit Hoskote

Intersection, Guild Art Gallery, Artists Centre, Mumbai. Curator: Ranjit Hoskote

1999

The First Fukuoka Asian Art Triennale, Fukuoka Asian Art Museum, Japan. Curator: Kuroda Raiji (cat.)

Nature Morte, Mary Place Gallery, Sydney. Curator: Peter Nagy

Embarkations, Sakshi Gallery, Mumbai. Curator: Yashodhara Dalmia (cat.)

Young Artists, National Gallery of Modern Art, Mumbai

1998

Art of the World 1998, Beaux Arts Magazine's international exhibition, Passage de Retz, Paris

Multimedia Art of the 90s, CIMA Gallery, Calcutta (cat.)

Jehangir Nicholson Collection, National Gallery of Modern Art, Mumbai

The Wilberding Collection, National Gallery of Modern Art, Mumbai

Indian Contemporary Art, Leverkusen and Monheim, Germany: The R.P.G. Collection (cat.)

SPIN, Sakshi Gallery, Mumbai

1997

Innenseite, Universität GhK, Kassel, Germany. Curator: Hamdi el Attar (cat.)

50 Years of Art in Mumbai, National Gallery of Modern Art, Mumbai

1996

Miniature Format Show, Sans Tache, Mumbai (cat.)

Monsoon Show, Jehangir Art Gallery, Mumbai

1995

Varsha '95, Y. B. Chavan Art Gallery, Mumbai

2011

Ernst, Sophie. "Public Notice 3: Jitish Kallat." *Take on Art Magazine* 1, 4 (2011).

Jumabhoy, Zehra. "Jitish Kallat: Mix and Match." *Time Out Mumbai*, March 19–31, 2011, pp. 18–20.

Ghose, Anindita. "Once upon a Moon." *HT Mint Lounge*, March 19, 2011, p. 17.

Wullschlager, Jackie. "Tate Britain's New Watercolour Exhibition." *FT.com*, February 18, 2011, http://www.ft.com/cms/s/2/894a2aa2-3ae3-11e0-8d81-00144feabdc0.html#axzz1EPYT1ka.

DiMeo, Mia. "108 Years Later." *ArtSlant.com*, January 31, 2011, http://www.artslant.com/chi/articles/show/21403.

2010

Snodgrass, Susan. "Reviews: Jitish Kallat." *Art in America Magazine*, December 1, 2010, http://www.art-inamerica.com/reviews/jitish-kallat/.

Raheja, Dinesh. "Contemporary Art by Jitish Kallat." *M Magazine*, December 2010.

Goldman, Edward. "The Three Best Museum Shows for This Thanksgiving Season." *HuffingtonPost.com*, November 19, 2010, http://www.huffingtonpost.com/edward-goldman/the-three-best-museum-sho_b_786200.html.

Connors, Thomas. "Public Notice 3: Visually Religious." *Indian Contemporary Art Journal* 2, 4 (2010).

McKean, Lise. "Stepping into the Past." *Art India* 15, 3 (2010).

Kurjakovic, Daniel. "The Layering of Unintended Meanings." *Burger Collection: Research Project "Quadrilogy" Theory/Conversations*, October 4, 2010.

Prakash, Chetna. "The Swami and the Stairway." *Times of India* (Crest Edition), October 2, 2010.

Ray, Sharmistha. "Artistic License." *Take on Art Magazine* 1, 2 (2010).

Sarma, Ramya. "Kallat Steps into Chicago." *Bengal Post*, September 5, 2010.

Ratnam, Dhamini. "In Light of Quite Another 9/11." *Hindustan Times* (Mumbai Edition), September 5, 2010.

Viera, Lauren. "Sept 11 1893, 2001 and Today." *Chicago Tribune*, September 9, 2010.

Sohal, Prabhjot. "Building Bridges." *Indian Express*, August 31, 2010.

Thomas, Sheena. "Art That Is Simply Terror-fic." *Mid-Day*, September 9, 2010.

Kulkarni, Reshma S. "A Global Cohesion." *Bombay Times*, September 9, 2010.

Geilert, Gerald. "The Astronomy of the Subway: Jitish Kallat in London." *Artconcerns.com*, June-July 2010, http://www.artconcerns.com/review.php?n=6.

Doshi, Riddhi. "Now, Jitish is a bone collector." *DNA—After hrs,* May 20, 2010.

Sarma, Ramya. "A Question of Life." *The Hindu*, May 30, 2010.

Ramanath, Renu. "The Empire Strikes Back and Jitish Kallat in London." *Art Concerns,* February-March 2010, http://www.artconcerns.com/html/article5Emperor.htm.

"Jitish Kallat." *Asian Art Newspaper* (February 2010), http://www.asianart-newspaper.com/article/jitish-kallat.

Davis, Brendan. Interview with Jitish Kallat. *ART Interview–Online Magazine* (Germany), February 5, 2010, http://www.art-interview.com/Issue_016/Issue_003/Issue_015/interview_Kallat_Jitish.html.

Sarma, Ramya. "Samosa X-rays in the Gallery." *Times of India* (Crest Edition), January 30, 2010.

2009

Fairley, Gina. "Navigating Contemporary India." *Asian Art News* 19, 3 (2009), pp. 92–96.

Sardesai, Abhay. "Variations on a Theme." *Art India* 14, 3 (September 2009), pp. 75–76.

Brigit, Sonna. "Unverfroren Hintergrundig Spirituell." *ART Das Kunstmagazin*, September 2009.

Cocteau, Jean. "Jitish Kallat: An Exclusive, Electronic Interview." *C Arts: Asian Contemporary Arts and Culture*, August 14, 2009, http://www.c-artsmag.com/articles/detail.php?Title=JITTISH%20KALLAT%20-%20An%20exclusive,electronic%20interview&ID_Comment=0.

Pillai, Varsha. "Two Sides to a Work of Art." *Jade*, May 2009.

Menon, Carroll Aarti. "Destiny's Child." *Economic Times*, May 29, 2009.

Von Bennigsen, Silvia, Irene Gludowacz, and Susanne Van Hagen. "Interview with Jitish Kallat." In *Global Art* (Hatje Cantz, 2009), pp. 36–43.

Dutta, Adip. "Ignited Minds." *Art India* 14, 2 (2009), p. 42.

2008

Shahane, Girish. "Jitish Kallat—Life, Death and the Struggle in Between." *Artist Profile*, no. 5 (2008), pp. 52–55.

Sharma, Shalini. "Kallat's Kaleidoscope." *Hi! Living*, October 2008.

Ananth, Deepak. "Indian Bazaar: Notes on Six Contemporary Indian Artists." *Flash Art* 41, 258 (July–September 2008), pp. 98–100.

Kallat, Jitish, and Shiladitya Sarkar. "When thoughts come with self-pasting adhesive…" *Art India* 13, 3/4 (September 2008), pp. 47–48.

Holmes, Pernilla. "Is Indian Art having an Indian Summer?" *Financial Times* (How To Spend It, London), August 2, 2008, pp. 6–9.

Nandwani, Deepali, "Jitish Kallat." *Man's World*, June 2008.

Ulmer, Brigitte. "Compressed Data from the Global Media Power." *NZZ Online* (Zurich), June 7, 2008.

Cruickshank, Alan. "Asian Attitudes." *Art & Australia,* 45, 3 (March-May 2008).

Harris, Lucian. "Feeding the Very Hungry God." *Art India* 13, 1 (March 2008), pp. 30–35.

Kallat, Jitish. "Art is Being Treated as an Asset Class." *Art Newspaper* 17, no. 189 (March 2008), p. 44.

Neal, Jane. "Jitish Kallat." *Modern Painters* 20, 1 (February 2008), pp. 95–96.

Shahane, Girish. "The Bone Collector." *Hi! BLITZ,* January 2008.

2007

Sarma, Ramya. "Blood, Sweat, and Cheers." *DNA Mumbai*, December 8, 2007.

Kallat, Jitish. "Heat and Dust." *Art India* 12, 4 (December 2007), pp. 120–21.

Munipalle, Vikas. "Sweet Memories." *Time Out Mumbai,* November 30–December 13, 2007.

Citron, Beth. "Jitish Kallat: Copyright 2007." *ART AsiaPacific*, no. 55 (October 2007), pp. 108–09.

McDonald, John. "Mumbai as a Modern Maxim." *Sydney Morning Herald*, February 2007, pp. 17–18.

 "Mumbai's Chaos in a Quiet Sydney Suburb." *Indian Link*, January 19, 2007.

2006

Hibberd, Lily. "Fifth Asia-Pacific Triennial APT5 Companion." *The Art Reader*, December 2006.

Carsley, Gary. "Bombay Blues" (review). *Art India* 11, 4 (2006), p. 106.

Sinha, Gayatri. "Politics of Waste, the Pool of Art!" *The Hindu*, January 2006.

2005

Dadyburjor, Farhad. "The Urban Space Mixed with Chaos Becomes My Muse." *DNA Mumbai*, December 2005.

Madhavan, Sangeetha and Marie Tan. "Life Culture." *Harpers Bazaar*, November 2005.

Dastur, Nicole. "Straight Answers." *Times of India*, September 2005.

Kapur, Rohini. "Public Notice: Art as Protest." *Hindustan Times* (HT Style), August 2005.

Terron, Simona. "On Acid Trip." *Times of India* (Westside Plus), May 2005.

Shahane, Girish. "Koffee with Kallat." *Time Out Mumbai,* March 2005.

Mendes, Sacha. "Poetry in Progress." *Elle*, February 2005.

Maddox, Georgina. "No Kidding." *Mumbai Newsline, The Indian Express*, February 2005.

Nooshaian, Tinaz. "Lord Ram Is on the Streets." *Asian Age*, February 2005.

Lee, Larry. "Jitish Kallat: The Lie of the Land." *ART AsiaPacific*, no. 43 (Winter 2005), pp. 81–82.

Sardesai, Abhay. "Orphans in the Storm." *Art India* 10, 2 (2005), p 14.

2004

Workman, Michael. "Jitish Kallat at Walsh Gallery." *Flash Art* 37 (November-December 2004), p. 49.

Camper, Fred. "War Against Terror" (review). *Art India* 10, 1 (2004).

2003

Hoskote, Ranjit. "Jitish Kallat." *Art AsiaPacific*, no. 37 (Winter 2003), pp. 52–54.

2002

Cotter, Holland. "First Information Report" (review). *New York Times*, October 18, 2002.

Mehta, Shireen. "Cerebral Strokes." *Verve*, July-September 2002.

2001

Chaturvedi, Bharati. "Metro Reflections." *Business Standard* (Leisure section, New Delhi), September 15–16, 2001.

Goel, Poonam. "Multiple Images Loom Large on His Canvas." *Hindustan Times* (HT City, Delhi), September 2001.

Dadachanji, Khushnuma. "For Kallat, Size does matter." *Times of India* (Bombay Times), August 30, 2001.

Maddox, Georgina. "Space Matters." *Mumbai Newsline, Indian Express,* August 30, 2001.

Hans Varghese, Mathews. "Feeling Young Man." *Art Frontline*, August 30, 2001.

VG, Jaideep. "Mortal Coils of a Double Helix and Search for Roots." *City Reporter*, June 2001.

Reddy, Anita. "Mixing Art with Science and Technology." *New Indian Express*, June 2001.

2000

Mehta, Anupa. "Ideas of Self and the Other." *Asian Art News*, November-December 2000).

Nowfaleena Ebrahim. "Young Talented and Famous." *Times of India* (Bombay Times), December 21, 2000.

Shah Verma, Jasmine. "Point of Reference." *Midday* (The List), December 2000.

Nagy, Peter. "An Artist of Confusion." *First City* (Delhi), February 2000.

1999

Shahane, Girish. "Images from Heaven." *Oomph! Art* (India), 1999.

Cotter, Holland. "Private Limited 1" (review). *New York Times*, November 24, 1999.

De, Ranjan. "Walls of a Diary." *Expressweek,* November 27, 1999.

Cohen, Andrew. "Contemporary Indian Painting: A Portfolio." *Art Journal* 58, 3 (October 1999), pp. 10–13.

Shah Varma, Jasmine. "Brushes with Paint." *Mid Day*, June 1999.

1998

Pinto, Jerry. "An Ordinary Recipe for a poster masquerading as an icon." *Kulture Bombay Times, The Times of India,* December 3, 1998.

Vijayan, Sarita. "Ce(re)brating Art!" *Inside Outside*, July 1998.

Vegas, Savia. "A Painter of Our Times." *Sunday Observer*, February 1998.

Ganesh, Shivani. "The Memory of an Elephant." *Island*, January 1998.

1996

Shahane, Girish. "The Intriguing Image." *Art India* 3, 2, 1996.

Mehta, Anupa. "The Artist as Inventor." *Art India*, October 1996.

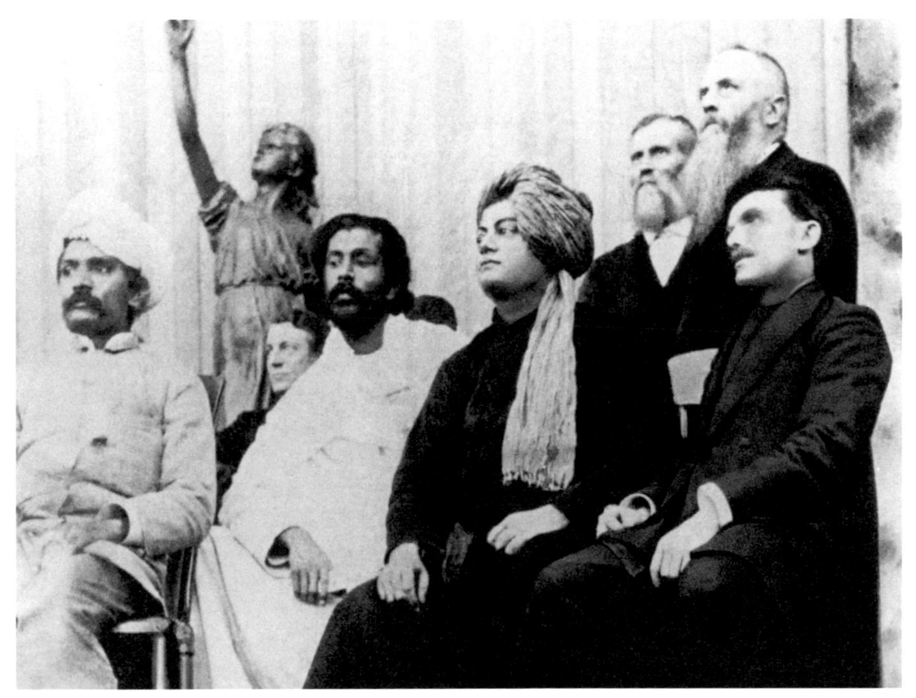

Swami Vivekananda (*center*), seated on the stage with other delegates to the World's Parliament of Religions, Chicago, in 1893.

WELCOME ADDRESS TO THE WORLD'S PARLIAMENT OF RELIGIONS, CHICAGO, SEPTEMBER 11, 1893

Sisters and Brothers of America,

It fills my heart with joy unspeakable to rise in response to the warm and cordial welcome which you have given us. I thank you in the name of the most ancient order of monks in the world; I thank you in the name of the mother of religions, and I thank you in the name of millions and millions of Hindu people of all classes and sects.

My thanks, also, to some of the speakers on this platform who, referring to the delegates from the Orient, have told you that these men from far-off nations may well claim the honor of bearing to different lands the idea of toleration. I am proud to belong to a religion which has taught the world both tolerance and universal acceptance. We believe not only in universal toleration, but we accept all religions as true. I am proud to belong to a nation which has sheltered the persecuted and the refugees of all religions and all nations of the earth. I am proud to tell you that we have gathered in our bosom the purest remnant of the Israelites, who came to Southern India and took refuge with us in the very year in which their holy temple was shattered to pieces by Roman tyranny. I am proud to belong to the religion which has sheltered and is still fostering the remnant of the grand Zoroastrian nation. I will quote to you, brethren, a few lines from a hymn which I remember to have repeated from my earliest boyhood, which is every day repeated by millions of human beings: "As the different streams having their sources in different places all mingle their water in the sea, so, O Lord, the different paths which men take through different tendencies, various though they appear, crooked or straight, all lead to Thee."

The present convention, which is one of the most august assemblies ever held, is in itself a vindication, a declaration to the world of the wonderful doctrine preached in the Gita: "Whosoever comes to Me, through whatsoever form, I reach him; all men are struggling through paths which in the end lead to me." Sectarianism, bigotry, and its horrible descendant, fanaticism, have long possessed this beautiful earth. They have filled the earth with violence, drenched it often and often with human blood, destroyed civilization and sent whole nations to despair. Had it not been for these horrible demons, human society would be far more advanced than it is now. But their time is come; and I fervently hope that the bell that tolled this morning in honor of this convention may be the death-knell of all fanaticism, of all persecutions with the sword or with the pen, and of all uncharitable feelings between persons wending their way to the same goal.

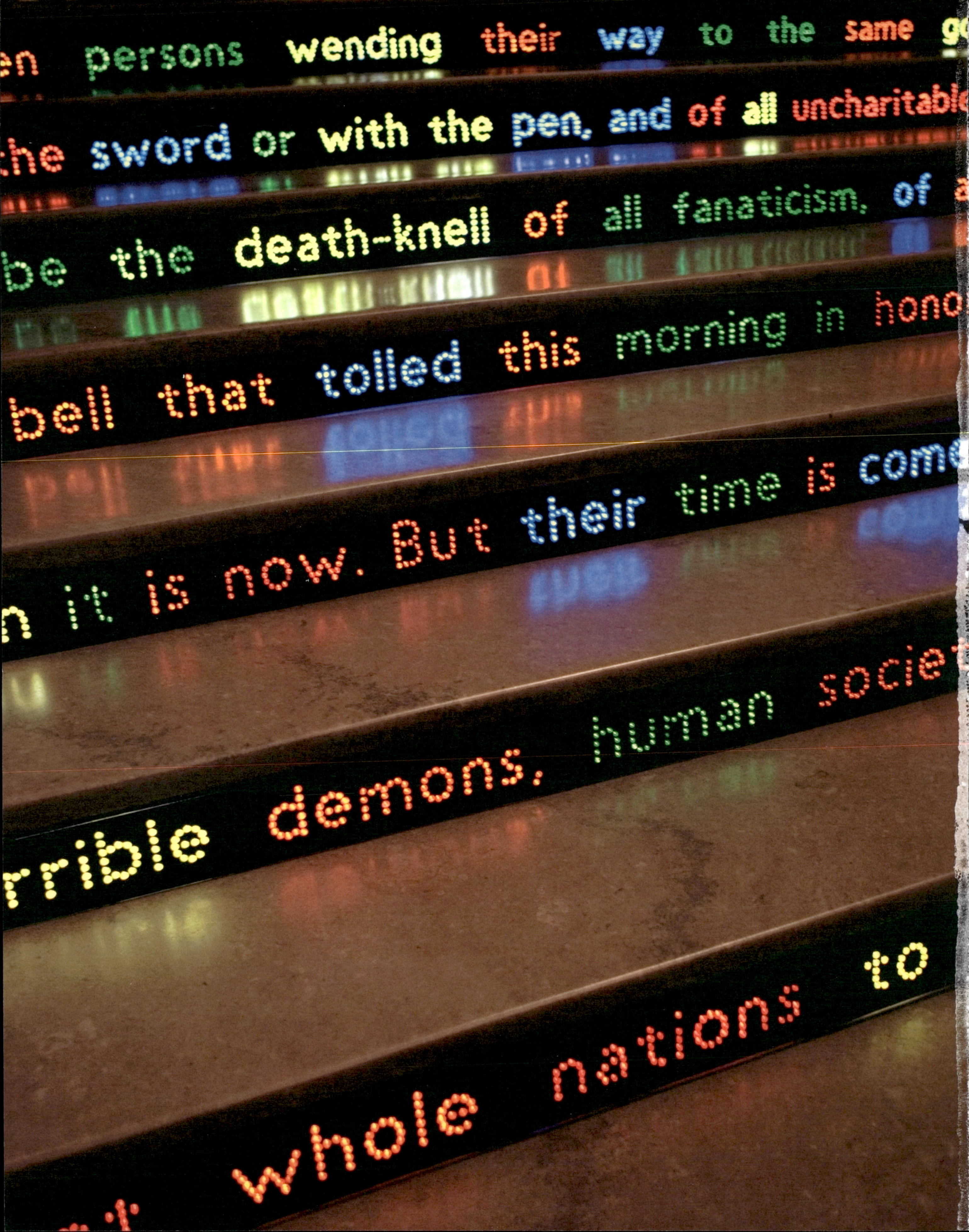

en persons wending their way to the same g

the sword or with the pen, and of all uncharitab

be the death-knell of all fanaticism, of

bell that tolled this morning in hono

n it is now. But their time is come

rrible demons, human socie

whole nations to